OUR PLANET EARTH

OUR Earth is made of layers of rock. The diagram below shows the Earth with a slice cut out. The hottest part is the core, at the centre. Around the core is the mantle.

The outer layer, the crust, is quite thin under the oceans, but it is thicker under the continents. Scientists now know that the Earth's crust is cracked, like the shell of a hard-boiled egg that has been dropped. The cracks are called faults. The huge sections of crust divided by the faults are called plates and they are moving very, very slowly. The continents have gradually moved across the Earth's surface as the crustal plates have moved. Sudden movements near the faults cause volcanic eruptions or earthquakes. Undersea earthquakes cause huge waves called tsunamis.

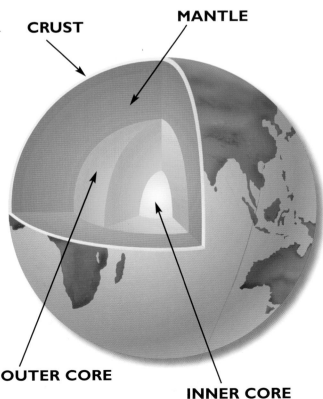

CRUST

MANTLE

OUTER CORE

INNER CORE

▲ *The Earth from space:* this satellite image shows Africa, Arabia, the Mediterranean Sea and Europe. The Sahara Desert has no cloud and is all sunny. Some of the white clouds near the Equator show where there are thunderstorms.

Can you name the oceans to the west (left) and to the east (right) of Africa? And can you name the continent – and the country – on the far west (left) of this image? (The maps on pages 7 and 8 will help you. Answers on page 96.)

FASCINATING FACTS ABOUT THE EARTH

DISTANCE AROUND THE EQUATOR 40,075 kilometres
DISTANCE AROUND THE POLES 40,007 kilometres
DISTANCE TO THE CENTRE OF THE EARTH 6370 kilometres
SURFACE AREA OF THE EARTH 510,065,600 square kilometres
PROPORTIONS OF SEA AND LAND 71% sea; 29% land
DISTANCE FROM THE EARTH TO THE SUN 150,000,000 kilometres
(It takes $8\frac{1}{2}$ minutes for the Sun's light to reach the Earth.)
DISTANCE FROM THE EARTH TO THE MOON 384,400 kilometres
THE EARTH TRAVELS AROUND THE SUN at 107,000 kilometres per hour, or nearly 30 kilometres per second
THE EARTH'S ATMOSPHERE is about 175 kilometres high
CHIEF GASES IN THE ATMOSPHERE Nitrogen 78%; oxygen 21%
AVERAGE DEPTH OF SEA 3900 metres
AVERAGE HEIGHT OF LAND 880 metres

Antoinette's

Children's
ATLAS

DAVID AND JILL WRIGHT

IN ASSOCIATION WITH
THE ROYAL GEOGRAPHICAL SOCIETY
WITH THE INSTITUTE OF BRITISH GEOGRAPHERS

CONTENTS

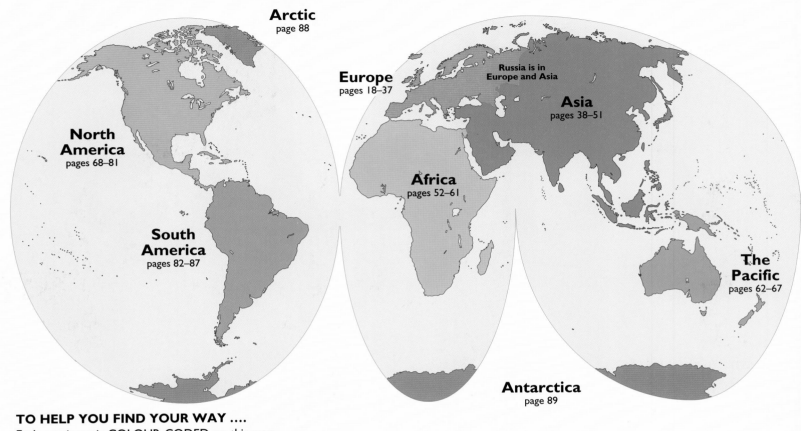

TO HELP YOU FIND YOUR WAY ....

Each continent is COLOUR-CODED on this map
AND on the contents page (opposite) AND on the heading of each atlas page.

TO RACHEL AND STEVEN

First published in Great Britain in 1987
by Philip's, a division of Octopus Publishing Group Limited
(www.octopusbooks.co.uk)
2–4 Heron Quays, London E14 4JP
An Hachette UK Company (www.hachettelivre.co.uk)

Twelfth edition 2007
Text © 1987, 2007 David and Jill Wright
Maps © 2007 Philip's
Reprinted 2009

Cartography by Philip's

A CIP catalogue record for this book is available from
the British Library.

ISBN 978–0–540–09005–1

Printed in Hong Kong

Details of other Philip's titles and services can be found
on our website at: **www.philips-maps.co.uk**

Philip's World Atlases are published in association with The Royal Geographical Society (with
The Institute of British Geographers).

The Society was founded in 1830 and given a
Royal Charter in 1859 for 'the advancement of
geographical science'. Today it is a leading world
centre for geographical learning – supporting
education, teaching, research and expeditions,
and promoting public understanding of the
subject.

Further information about the Society and
how to join may be found on its website at:
www.rgs.org

ABOUT THIS ATLAS

Philip's Children's Atlas is written by
people who enjoy learning about our
wonderful world and want others to
enjoy it, too.

David and Jill Wright have taught
geography in schools and colleges. We
have visited more than a hundred
countries to understand the scenery and
people better and to take photographs.
Some of these visits have been made
with our own children or with student
groups. This has helped us to see the
world through children's eyes.

There is so much we want to tell you
about, and so little space. We have had
to choose what to write about and what
to leave out – very hard! So we hope this
atlas will help YOU, the reader, to begin
a life-long exploration of the world, to
notice all the links we have with all parts
of the world, and to find out more from
other books and websites.

The Earth travels round the Sun in 365¼ days, which we call a year. Every four years we add an extra day to February to use up the ¼ days. This is called a Leap Year. The Earth travels at a speed of over 107,000 kilometres an hour. (You have travelled 600 kilometres through space while reading this!)

The Earth also spins round and round as it travels through space. It spins round once in 24 hours, which

we call a day. Places on the Equator are spinning at 1660 kilometres an hour. Because of the way the Earth moves, we experience day and night, and different seasons during a year (see page 13). No part of our planet is too hot or too cold for life to survive. Yet the Earth is 150 million kilometres from the Sun.

The Moon is our nearest neighbour in space. It is 384,400 kilometres away. The first men to reach the

Moon took four days to travel there in 1969. On the way, they took many photos of the Earth, such as the one on the left. The Earth looks very blue from space because of all the sea. It is the only planet in the Solar System with sea. Look at the swirls of cloud. These show that the Earth has an atmosphere. Our atmosphere contains oxygen and water vapour, and it keeps all living things alive.

EARTH FROM SPACE

▼ *Glaciers in the Himalayas,* *as can be seen from space. The white stripes are glaciers, or 'rivers of ice' in the valleys. There is snow on the mountains.*

▶ *The Great Lakes* *from space. Look at the map on page 75 to find their names. On the east (right) is the Atlantic Ocean.*

▼ *Europe at night.* *The lights from cities, towns and villages will help you spot Britain, Spain and Italy. Now look at the map on page 19.*

▼ *Clouds and smoke over Italy.* *The white patches are clouds, but look for the brown smoke. This comes from Mount Etna: a volcano on the island of Sicily.*

MOUNTAINS, PLAINS AND SEAS

THE map shows that there is much more sea than land in the world. Over two-thirds of the Earth's surface is covered with water or ice. The Pacific is by far the biggest ocean; the map splits it in two.

The mountains are shown with shadows on this map. Look for the world's highest mountain range – the Himalayas, in Asia. There are high mountains on the western side of both American continents. Most of the world's great mountain ranges have been made by folding in the Earth's crust.

The green expanse across northern Europe and northern Asia is the world's biggest plain.

▲ *The Atlantic Ocean* washes the desert shore of Namibia, in southern Africa.

▲ *Mountains and plains* – and a vicuña. In which country does this animal live? (Answer on page 96.)

▲ *Farming the Great Plains of North America.* The Plains cover large areas of the USA and Canada. This land in Alberta, Canada, has just been harvested. The almost flat land of the Great Plains ends where the Rocky Mountains begin.

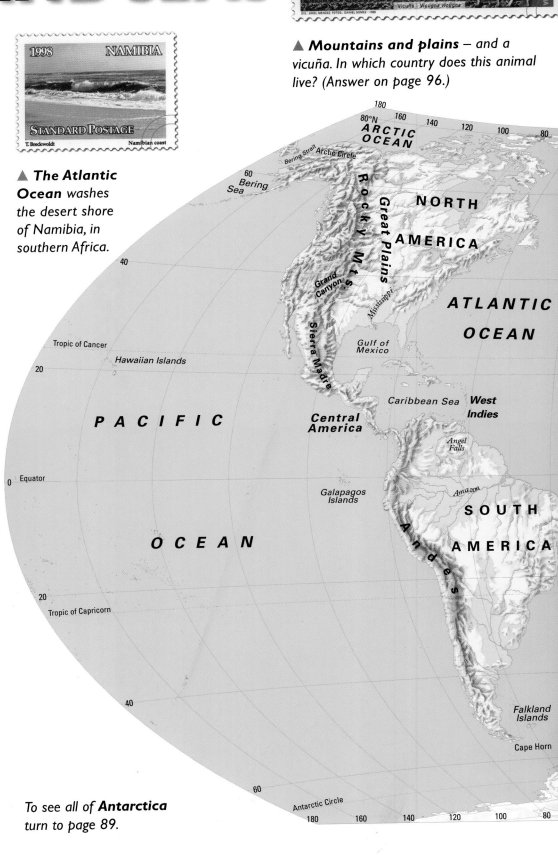

To see all of **Antarctica** turn to page 89.

WORLD RECORDS: LARGEST • LONGEST • HIGHEST • DEEPEST

LARGEST OCEAN Pacific, 169,500,000 sq km

DEEPEST PART OF OCEANS Mariana Trench, 11,022 metres (Pacific)

LARGEST LAKE Caspian Sea, 371,000 sq km (Europe and Asia)

DEEPEST LAKE Lake Baikal, 1620 metres (Russia)

LONGEST RIVERS Nile, 6800 km (Africa); Amazon, 6450 km (South America); Yangtze, 6380 km (Asia)

LARGEST ISLANDS Australia, 7,741,220 sq km; Greenland, 2,175,600 sq km

LARGEST DESERT Sahara, 9,100,000 sq km (Africa)

HIGHEST MOUNTAIN Everest, 8850 m (Asia)

LONGEST MOUNTAIN RANGE Andes, 7200 km (South America)

LONGEST GORGE Grand Canyon, 446 km (North America)

HIGHEST WATERFALL Angel Falls, 979 metres (Venezuela, South America)

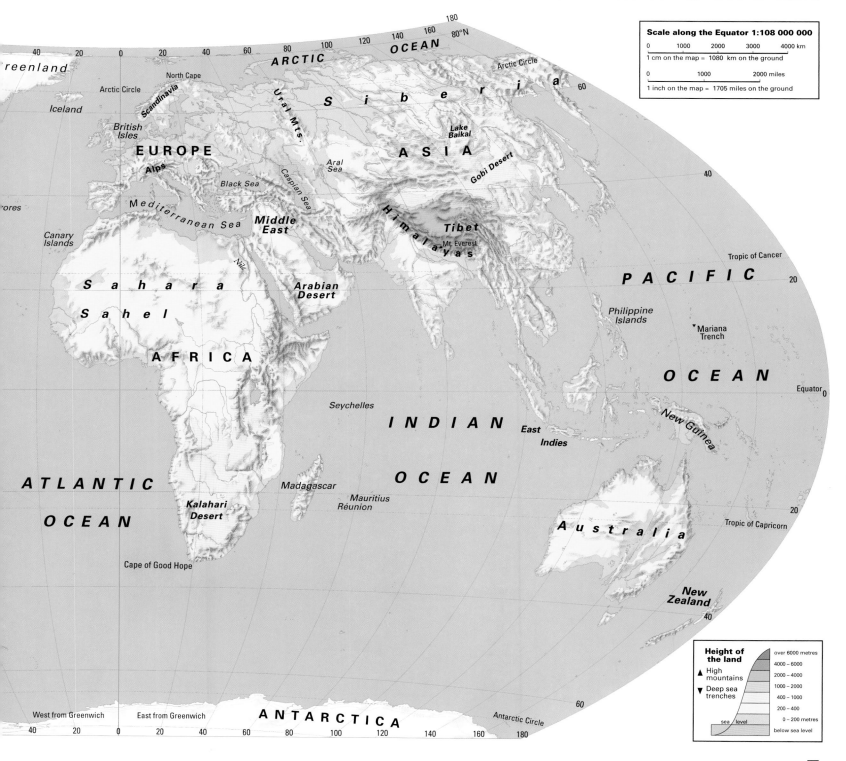

Scale along the Equator 1:108 000 000

0   1000   2000   3000   4000 km

1 cm on the map = 1080 km on the ground

0   1000   2000 miles

1 inch on the map = 1705 miles on the ground

Height of the land
▲ High mountains
▼ Deep sea trenches

over 6000 metres
4000 – 6000
2000 – 4000
1000 – 2000
400 – 1000
200 – 400
0 – 200 metres
sea level
below sea level

THE COUNTRIES OF THE WORLD

A D-I-Y QUIZ

On this map, some small countries are labelled with only the first few letters of their name. Try to guess the whole name. Then check your answers on the continent maps: *Europe page 19; Asia page 39; Africa page 53; Pacific pages 62–63; West Indies page 81; South America page 83.*

FIVE of the continents of the world are divided into countries.

Look at the boundaries between countries: they have all been decided by people. Some follow natural features, such as rivers or mountain ranges. But some boundaries separate people of the same language, and this can cause problems.

This map has been drawn to show each country at the correct size. So you can see which countries are big, which are middle-sized and which are small. But because the sizes are correct, some of the shapes are not quite right. To see **both** correct size **and** correct shape we all need to look at a globe.

▲ *The European Union –* a map on a stamp from a member country. Which one? (See page 96.)

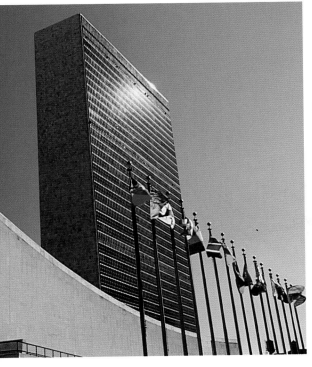

▲ *The United Nations building, in New York City, USA. The world's problems are discussed here – and sometimes solved. Look at the flag (right): what do you think the symbols mean? (Answer on page 96.)*

▼ *The United Nations flag.*

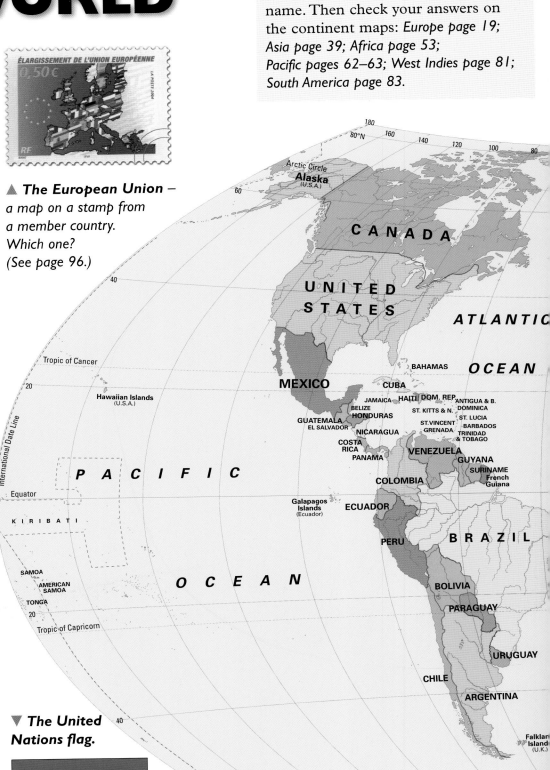

WHICH ARE THE WORLD'S BIGGEST COUNTRIES?

Only five of the 'top ten' countries with large populations are also among the 'top ten' biggest countries.

TOP TEN COUNTRIES BY SIZE (SQUARE KILOMETRES)			
1. Russia	17,075,400	6. Australia	7,741,220
2. Canada	9,970,610	7. India	3,287,263
3. USA	9,629,091	8. Argentina	2,780,400
4. China	9,596,961	9. Kazakhstan	2,724,900
5. Brazil	8,514,215	10. Sudan	2,505,813

TOP TEN COUNTRIES BY POPULATION (U.N. FIGURES)			
1. China	1314 million	6. Pakistan	166 million
2. India	1095 million	7. Bangladesh	147 million
3. USA	298 million	8. Russia	143 million
4. Indonesia	245 million	9. Nigeria	132 million
5. Brazil	188 million	10. Japan	127 million

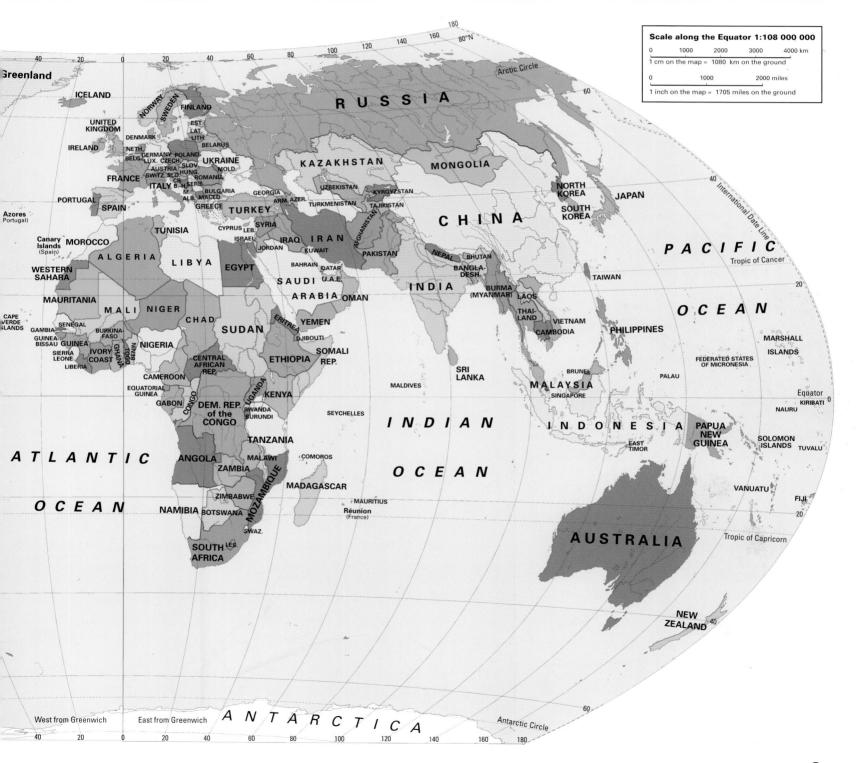

Scale along the Equator 1:108 000 000

0   1000   2000   3000   4000 km

1 cm on the map = 1080 km on the ground

0   1000   2000 miles

1 inch on the map = 1705 miles on the ground

PEOPLE OF THE WORLD

THERE is *one* race of people: the human race. In Latin, we are all known as *Homo sapiens* – 'wise person'. The differences between people, such as dark or light skin, hair and eyes, are small.

The smaller map (below) shows the rich and the poor countries of the world. In any one country there are rich and poor people, but the difference between countries is even greater.

The map shows that the richest countries are in North America, Europe, Japan and Australia. Here most people usually have plenty to eat. They can buy many kinds of food; they can go to a doctor or hospital when they need to, and the children can go to school.

The richest countries are the ones that control most of the world's trade and make decisions about international rules. But they also give aid to help the poorer countries.

The poorest countries (shown in dark green) are in the tropics – mostly in Africa. Life in these countries is very different from life in the rich world. Many people struggle to grow enough food, and they are often hungry.

People who do not have enough to eat find it difficult to work hard and they get ill more easily. They do not have enough money to pay for medicines or to send their children to school to learn to read and write. Some of the poorest people live in shanty towns in or near large cities.

But many people in the tropics do manage to break out of this 'cycle of poverty'. They now have a better diet, and more and more people can obtain clean water. Primary schools now teach most children to read and write and do simple arithmetic – though there are few books and classes may be very large. In many places, village health workers are taught to recognize and treat the common diseases.

▲ **Crowded and poor: a shanty town in Brazil.** *These shanties on a steep hillside in Rio de Janeiro were built by people who have nowhere else to live. Some of them have low-paid jobs, but others have to beg to get enough to eat.*

THIRD WORLD AID

Watering onions in The Gambia, West Africa. This boy's watering-can was given by a charity to help the family grow more food. The onions can be sold to people living in the city. Many schemes like this are helped by money given by the rich countries of the world.

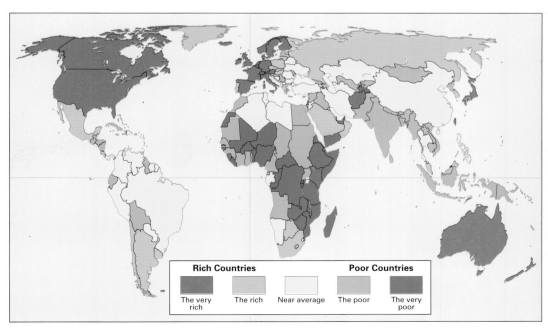

Rich Countries			Poor Countries	
The very rich	The rich	Near average	The poor	The very poor

The map below shows where the world's people live. The darker the colour, the more people there are. Most of the world has very few people: the cream or yellow areas.

The areas with few people are mostly desert, or high mountains, or dense forests, or very cold. Over half the world's people live in the lowlands of south and east Asia.

Other crowded areas are parts of Europe and the Nile Valley. The most crowded places of all are the big cities. Find the cities with more than 10 million people on the map.

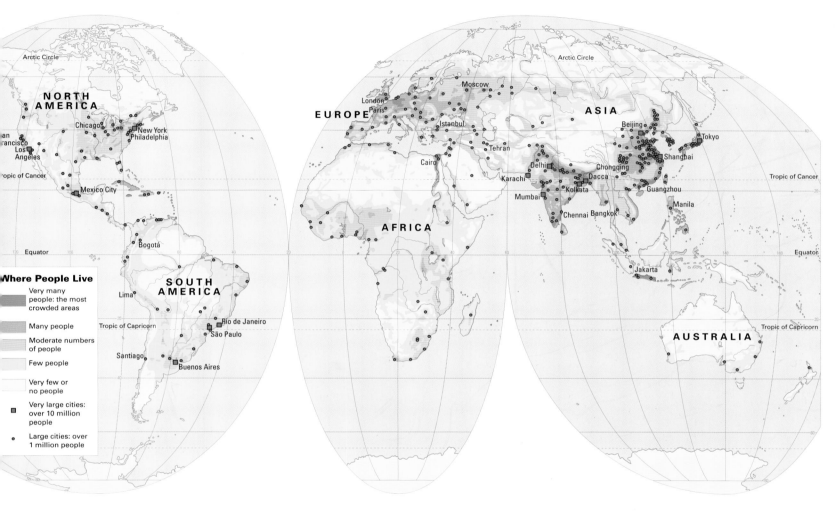

Where People Live

- Very many people: the most crowded areas
- Many people
- Moderate numbers of people
- Few people
- Very few or no people
- ■ Very large cities: over 10 million people
- • Large cities: over 1 million people

▲ **Empty and poor:** *a Tuareg nomad living in the Sahara desert, in Mali. It is hot and dusty and life is hard. The nomads move around with their animals.*

▲ **Crowded and rich:** *the skyscrapers of 'downtown' Seattle, a city in the north-west of the USA. In the distance are the leafy suburbs, overlooked by Mount Rainier, an old volcano. The USA is the world's richest country, but there are poor people living in some areas of the cities.*

COLD AND HOT LANDS

FIVE important lines are drawn across these maps of the world: the Arctic and Antarctic Circles; the Tropics of Cancer and Capricorn; and the Equator. They divide the world roughly into *polar*, *temperate* and *tropical* zones.

The *polar* lands remain cold all through the year, even though the summer days are long and some snow melts.

The *temperate* lands have four seasons: summer and winter, with spring and autumn in between. But these seasons come at different times of the year north and south of the Equator. June is midwinter in southern lands.

The *tropical* lands are always hot, except where mountains or plateaus reach high above sea level. For some of the year the sun is directly overhead at noon (local time). Look at the RED area on the maps.

The map on THIS page shows the world in June. Hardly anywhere is very cold (except for Antarctica in midwinter, of course). Most of the very hot areas in June are NORTH of the Equator.

The December map (opposite page) is very different. Both Canada and Russia are VERY cold. Most of the hottest areas in December are SOUTH of the Equator, near the Tropic of Capricorn, because December is midsummer.

▲ **Arctic winter.** *Winter begins early in Greenland. This fishing boat is frozen in the harbour at Angmagssalik, near the Arctic Circle. There are 24 hours of dark and cold at Christmas. Yet by June, the ice will have melted, and there will be 24 hours of daylight.*

DID YOU KNOW?

Children in New Zealand open their Christmas presents in midsummer.

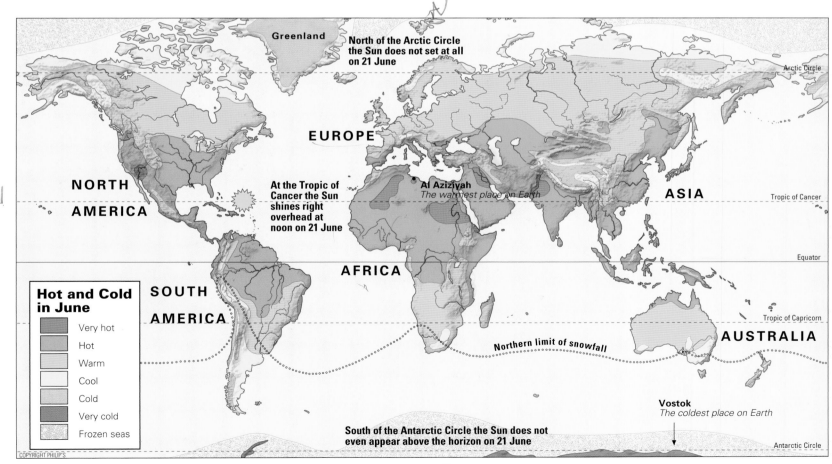

Greenland

North of the Arctic Circle the Sun does not set at all on 21 June

Arctic Circle

EUROPE

NORTH AMERICA

At the Tropic of Cancer the Sun shines right overhead at noon on 21 June

Al Aziziyah
The warmest place on Earth

ASIA

Tropic of Cancer

AFRICA

Equator

Hot and Cold in June

SOUTH AMERICA

Tropic of Capricorn

AUSTRALIA

Northern limit of snowfall

- Very hot
- Hot
- Warm
- Cool
- Cold
- Very cold
- Frozen seas

Vostok
The coldest place on Earth

South of the Antarctic Circle the Sun does not even appear above the horizon on 21 June

Antarctic Circle

COPYRIGHT PHILIP'S

12

COLD & HOT LANDS FACTS

HOTTEST RECORDED TEMPERATURE
58°C at Al Aziziyah in Libya
COLDEST RECORDED TEMPERATURE
−89.2°C at Vostok in Antarctica
**GREATEST CHANGE OF TEMPERATURE
AT ONE PLACE IN A YEAR**
From −70°C to +36.7°C at
Verkhoyansk in Siberia, Russia

▲ *In the hot, wet tropics, trees
grow tall and ferns grow fast. It is all
green – and quite dark – in this forest
on the island of Tobago, in the West Indies
(see page 81).*

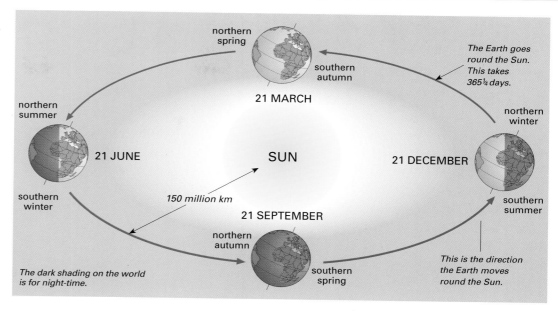

The seasons are different north and south of the Equator. In June it is
summer in North America, Europe and Asia. The sun is overhead at the
Tropic of Cancer. The North Pole is tilted towards the sun, and the Arctic
enjoys 24 hours of daylight. Notice that Antarctica is in total darkness.

By December, the Earth has travelled halfway round the sun. The sun is
overhead at the Tropic of Capricorn. The South Pole is tilted towards the sun.
Antarctica now has 24 hours of daylight, and it is summer in South America,
southern Africa and Australia.

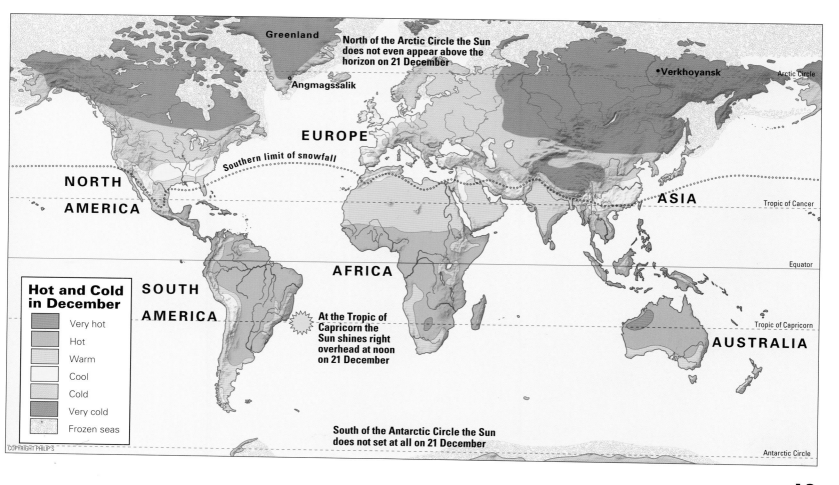

WET AND DRY LANDS

WATER is needed by all living things. But different parts of the world receive different amounts of water.

Follow the Equator on these two maps: the dark blue colour (below) shows heavy rain. Thick tropical forest grows here (page 15).

Now find the Tropics of Cancer and Capricorn: many parts are dry all year, and there are big deserts. Between the tropical forests and the deserts, there are 'savanna' areas, with tall grass and bushes: these areas have a wet and a dry season.

North of the Sahara Desert, near the Mediterranean Sea, it rains in winter. Summers are hot and dry.

In temperate lands, places near the oceans receive rain from the damp winds that blow from the sea all year. Trees grow well here. Far inland, it is much drier and there are vast grasslands, like the prairies of North America and the Russian steppes. In the centre of Asia, there is a desert with very cold winters.

Further north, temperate forests of pines and firs stretch right across North America, Europe and Asia.

In the far north, there is 'tundra', with no trees. The land is snow-covered for many months in winter, and marshy in the short summer.

Finally, Greenland and Antarctica are mostly snow and ice: find them on pages 88 and 89.

▲ **Forest and mountains in Alberta, Canada.** *The coniferous trees can survive Canada's bitterly cold winters. In the high mountains, trees cannot grow: it is too cold and the soil is too thin. Can you see the forest across the lake?*

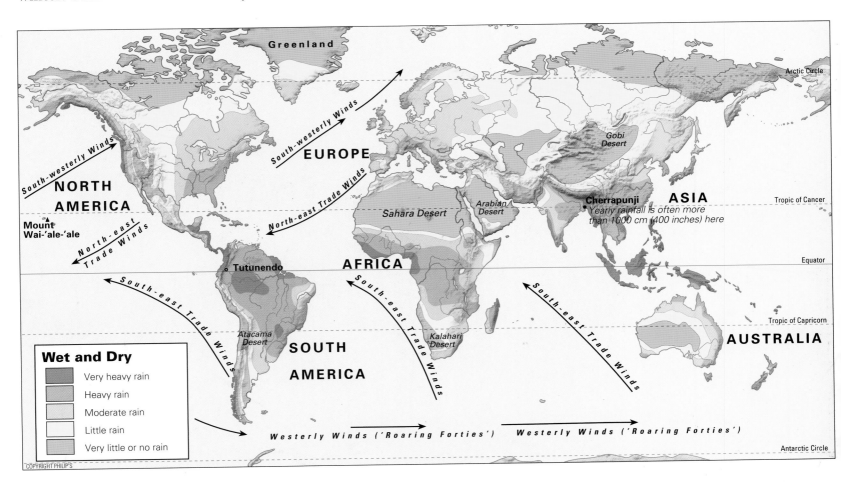

Wet and Dry
- Very heavy rain
- Heavy rain
- Moderate rain
- Little rain
- Very little or no rain

COPYRIGHT PHILIP'S

HIGHEST RAINFALL IN ONE MONTH
9299 mm in one month at Cherrapunji, India

HIGHEST RAINFALL IN ONE YEAR
26,461 mm in one year at Cherrapunji

MOST RAINY DAYS
350 days in a year at Mount Wai-'ale-'ale in Hawaii

WETTEST PLACE ON AVERAGE
Over 11 metres of rain a year at Tutunendo, Colombia

DRIEST PLACE In the Atacama Desert, northern Chile: no rain for 400 years!

This map shows NATURAL vegetation – but in many places people have cut down forests to make farmland and towns. Most scientists now believe that pollution is changing the climates of the world: we can expect more storms, more floods, more droughts (lack of rain) and hotter temperatures in most places. As sea level rises, the lowest land near the sea is at risk from floods.

▲ **Burning the savanna, in northern Ghana, West Africa.** *At the end of the long dry season, farmers burn the bush (long grass and small trees). The land will be ready for planting crops when it rains. Sometimes, lightning can cause fires.*

▲ **Sand dunes in the desert in Namibia, southern Africa.** *The Namib Desert has given its name to the country of Namibia. It is a very dry area, west of the Kalahari Desert. But most of the world's desert areas are rocky, not sandy.*

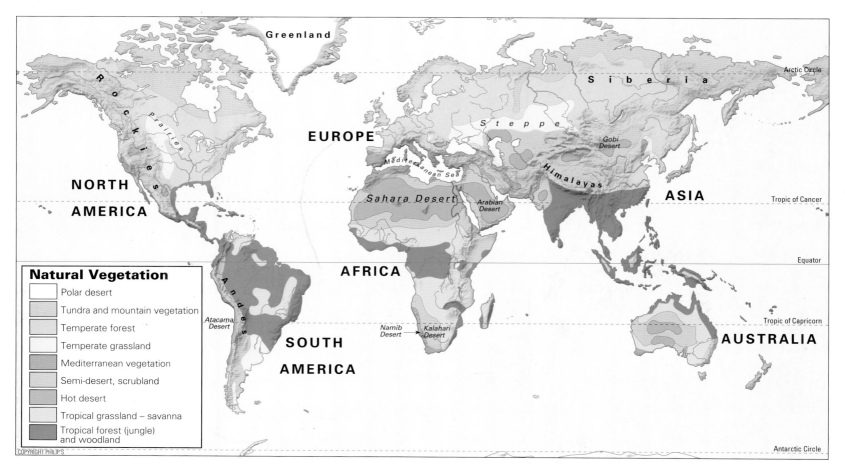

Natural Vegetation

- Polar desert
- Tundra and mountain vegetation
- Temperate forest
- Temperate grassland
- Mediterranean vegetation
- Semi-desert, scrubland
- Hot desert
- Tropical grassland – savanna
- Tropical forest (jungle) and woodland

COPYRIGHT PHILIP'S

ENJOYING MAPS

AN atlas is a book of maps. The maps in this book have been carefully drawn by cartographers (map-makers) to tell us about the countries of the world.

The maps on pages 6 to 15 show the whole world. Because the world is round, the best model is a globe. It is impossible to draw a really accurate map of the round world on a flat piece of paper. That is why the Pacific Ocean is cut in half, and Antarctica becomes a long thin strip. On pages 88 and 89 there are maps of parts of the world viewed from a different angle.

The maps on pages 18 to 89 show the continents and countries of the world. Each map has a key, with information that will help you 'read' the map. Use your imagination to 'see' what the land is like in each part of the world that you visit through these pages. The photos and text will make your picture clearer.

These two pages explain the key to all the maps. The country of GHANA is used as an example. Ghana is in square B2 of the map (right). Find ⓑ at the top of the map with one finger, and ➋ at the side of the map with another finger. Move each finger in the direction of the arrows; Ghana is where they meet.

The capital city of each country is underlined on the maps. The rulers of the country live in the capital city, and it is the biggest city in most countries. But not all capital cities are big. On this map, you can see three sizes of city. The biggest ones are marked by a square; they have over one million people. Middle-sized cities have a big circle, and smaller cities have a small circle. Small towns and villages are not shown on maps of this scale, but some have been included in this atlas because they are mentioned in the text.

▲ *The border between Ghana and Burkina Faso. The red lines on the map show the boundaries between countries. When travelling from one country to another, you have to stop at the border. These children live in Ghana and their flag flies on their side of the border.*

'BYE-BYE SAFE JOURNEY' is the message on the arch. In Ghana, most officials speak English. In Burkina Faso officials speak French.

POSTAGE STAMPS ... are on many pages of this atlas

You can learn so much from stamps! The map shows you that Ghana is a country; the stamps tell you the official language of Ghana, and show you Ghana's flag.

The map tells you that Ghana has a coastline; the 10Np stamp tells you the name of Ghana's main port, and shows you the big modern cranes there.

The map shows that this port is very near to Accra, which is the capital city of Ghana.

The map tells you the name of Ghana's biggest lake (man-made). The 6Np stamp shows you the dam and its name.

You can see that they chose the narrowest part of the valley to build the dam. On page 57, there is a picture of a ferry on the lake.

COINS OF THE WORLD

The **Ghana coin** (left) shows cocoa pods growing on the branches of a cocoa tree. Cocoa is a major export from Ghana. Another Ghana coin (right) shows traditional drums.

Other countries also picture familiar items on their coins. **Nigeria** has a palm tree on its coins; **The Gambia** has a sailing ship on one of its coins (see page 53).

But don't believe everything you find on coins: there is a LION on the 10p UK coin!

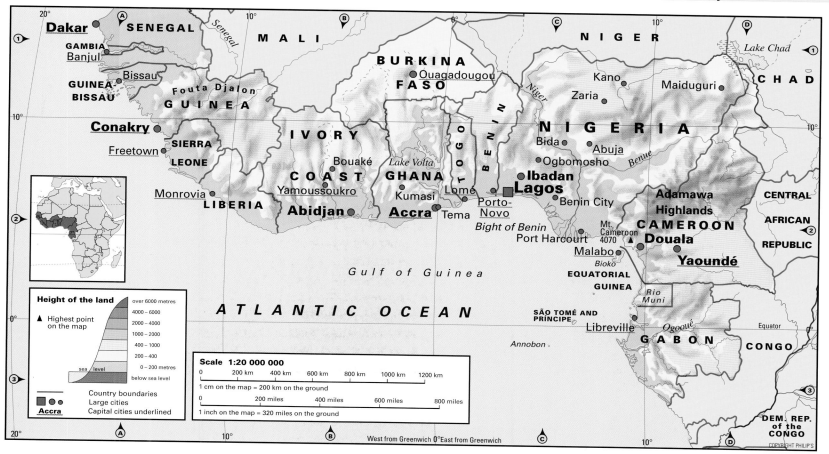

HEIGHT OF THE LAND

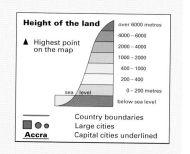

The countries of West Africa are coloured so that you can tell the height of the land. Green shows the lowest land. Often the real land will not look green – in the dry season the grass is brown. The higher land is coloured brown, even though some parts are covered with thick green forest!

The highest point in West Africa is shown with a small black triangle – find it in square C2. And to find land below sea level, try page 25. In West Africa, Cameroon has some dramatic mountains, but elsewhere the change from lowland to highland is often quite gentle. The 'shadows' on the map help you to see which mountains have steep slopes.

Blue means water: the oceans, big rivers and lakes. Their names are in *italic print*, such as *Lake Volta*. Blue dashes show rivers which dry up in some years.

SCALE

This box shows the scale of the map. The scale can be written in different ways. The map is drawn to a scale of 1:20,000,000, which means that the distance between two places on the ground is exactly 20 million times bigger than it is on this page! Other maps in this atlas are drawn to different scales: little Belgium (page 25) is drawn at a scale of 1:2 million, while the largest country in the world is drawn at a scale of 1:45 million (Russia, page 41). Another way of writing the scale of this map is to say that 1 centimetre on the map is equal to 200 kilometres on the ground in West Africa.

You can use the scale line to make your own scale ruler. Put the straight edge of a strip of paper against the scale line and mark the position of 0, 200, 400, 600 kilometres, etc. Carefully number each mark. Now move your scale ruler over the map to see how far it is between places. For example, Accra to Abidjan is 400 kilometres.

EUROPE

THE map shows the great North European Plain that stretches from the Atlantic Ocean to Russia. This plain has most of Europe's best farmland, and many of the biggest cities.

To the north of the plain are the snowy mountains of Scandinavia. To the south are even higher mountains: the Pyrenees, the Alps and Carpathians, and the Caucasus Mountains. Southern Europe has hills and mountains by the Mediterranean Sea. The small areas of lowland are carefully farmed.

PUZZLE

The most important building in Europe?
● *Where is it found?*
(Answer on page 96.)

EUROPE FACTS

AREA 10,531,000 sq km (including European Russia). Europe is the smallest continent.
HIGHEST POINT Mt Elbrus (Russia), 5642 metres
LOWEST POINT By Caspian Sea, minus 38 metres
LONGEST RIVER Volga (Russia), 3690 km
LARGEST LAKE Caspian Sea*, 371,000 sq km
BIGGEST COUNTRY Russia*, 17,075,400 sq km (total area – Europe and Asia)
BIGGEST ALL-EUROPEAN COUNTRY Ukraine, 603,700 sq km
SMALLEST COUNTRY Vatican City* (in Rome, Italy), less than half a square kilometre!
MOST CROWDED COUNTRY Malta
LEAST CROWDED COUNTRY Iceland
* A world record as well as a European record

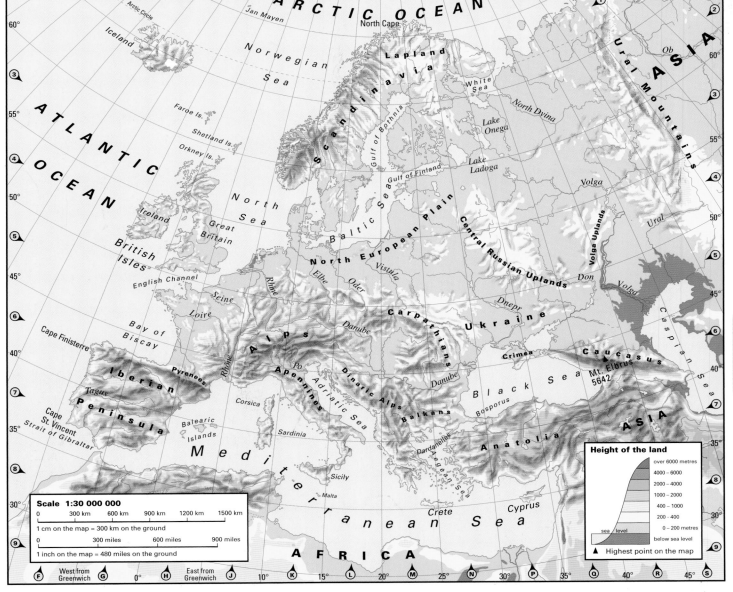

These stamps are from countries that are in the European Union. Can you name them? (Answers on page 96.)

▲ **Northern Europe: Iceland.** *Lake Jokulsarlon has many small icebergs which break off the glacier that comes from the ice-cap. Ice melts to make the lake.*

▲ **Central Europe: Austria.** *These high mountains are called the Alps. In winter, there will be snow here. In summer, the grass is for the cows – can you see any?*

▲ **Southern Europe: Sardinia.** *The island of Sardinia is part of Italy and is in the Mediterranean. It is very hot and dry in the summer. It is popular for holidays.*

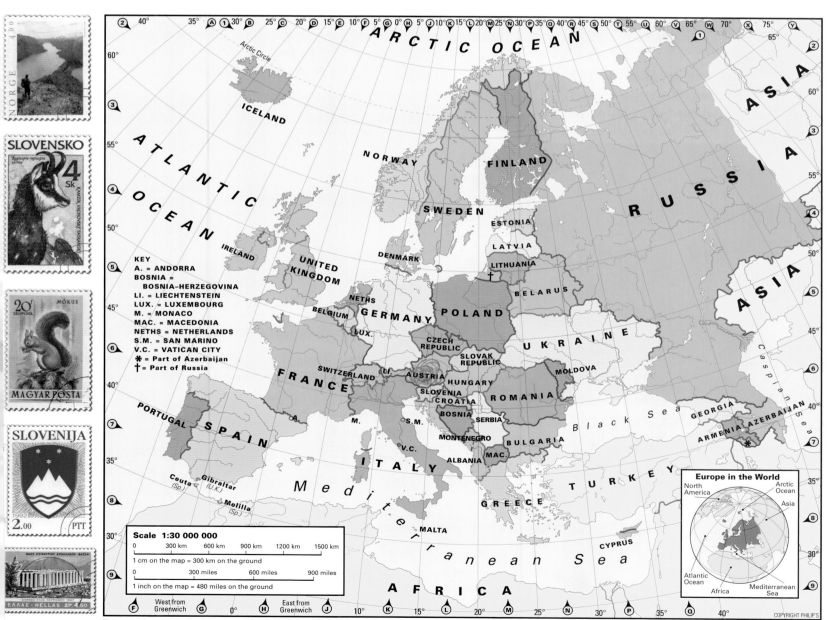

KEY
A. = ANDORRA
BOSNIA = BOSNIA–HERZEGOVINA
LI. = LIECHTENSTEIN
LUX. = LUXEMBOURG
M. = MONACO
MAC. = MACEDONIA
NETHS = NETHERLANDS
S.M. = SAN MARINO
V.C. = VATICAN CITY
* = Part of Azerbaijan
† = Part of Russia

Scale 1:30 000 000

0   300 km   600 km   900 km   1200 km   1500 km

1 cm on the map = 300 km on the ground

0   300 miles   600 miles   900 miles

1 inch on the map = 480 miles on the ground

West from Greenwich   0°   East from Greenwich

Europe in the World

The countries of Georgia, Armenia and Azerbaijan are really in Asia but are also included on this map because they are at a larger scale.

COPYRIGHT PHILIP'S

THE UK AND IRELAND

THE United Kingdom (UK) is made up of Great Britain (England, Wales and Scotland) and Northern Ireland.

The UK was the most important country in the world 150 years ago. Many old factories and coal mines have now closed down, but new factories have been built.

Much of the UK is still quiet and beautiful, with very varied scenery. The north and west of Great Britain are made of old, hard rocks. This area is higher and wetter than the south and east, and has pasture for cattle and sheep. Most of the arable farming is in the lower, drier and flatter south and east.

▲ **Bodiam Castle** is in the county of Sussex, south of London. It was built over 600 years ago against a possible French invasion. Today it is a ruin surrounded by a fine moat and its 'invaders' are tourists. The tourist industry is very important for the UK, and visitors come from all over the world to visit historic places.

▲ **Horse-power:**
Long ago, horses were used for ploughing the fields – a skilled job. But today, 'horse-power' means petrol and machines.

▲ **Rugby football** was invented in the 19th century by a schoolboy at an English private school at Rugby. It is very popular in Wales – important games are played in Cardiff's Millennium Stadium.

▲ **Dublin, capital of the Republic of Ireland.** This air-photo shows us that Dublin is built on both sides of the River Liffey. How many bridges can you see? A quarter of the country's population lives in Dublin and its suburbs.

▲ **The Somerset Levels,** south of Bristol in south-west England. The foreground was marshland which has been drained – it is below the level of high tides.

The Republic of Ireland is a completely separate country from the UK. Its money is now the Euro. There were twice as many people in Ireland 150 years ago as there are today. Farming is still important, but new factories have been built in many towns. Even so, many Irish people have moved to the UK or to the USA to find work.

Can you find these on the map?
Highest mountain – Ben Nevis
Longest river – Shannon
Largest lake – Lough Neagh
Greenwich Meridian – 0°

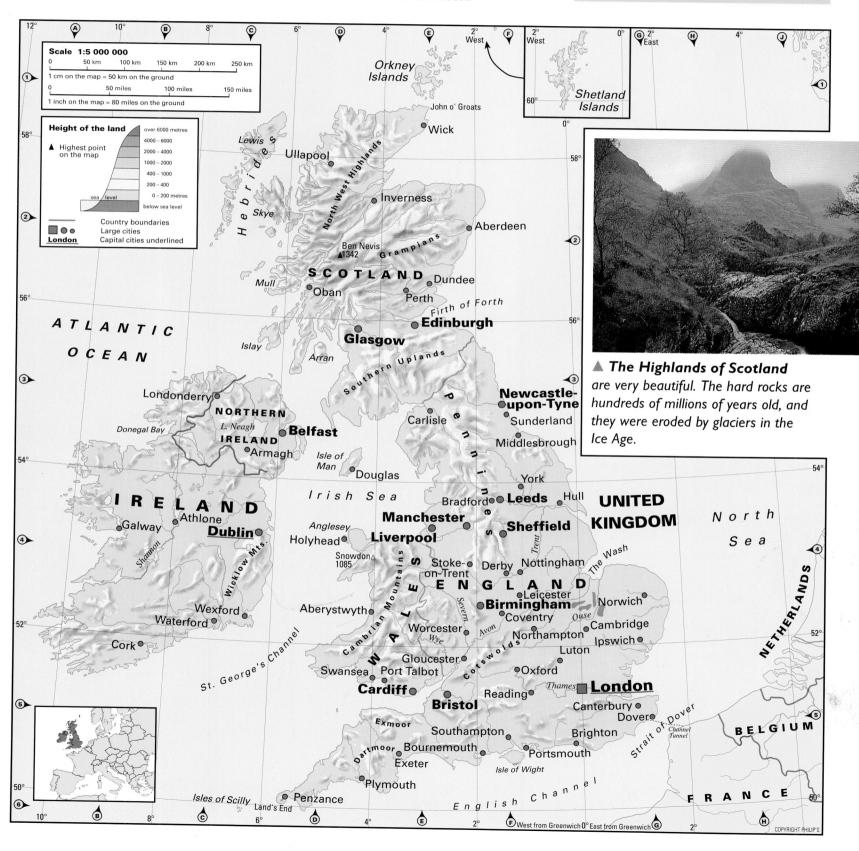

Scale 1:5 000 000

0   50 km   100 km   150 km   200 km   250 km
1 cm on the map = 50 km on the ground
0   50 miles   100 miles   150 miles
1 inch on the map = 80 miles on the ground

Height of the land
over 6000 metres
4000 – 6000
2000 – 4000
1000 – 2000
400 – 1000
200 – 400
0 – 200 metres
sea level
below sea level
▲ Highest point on the map

Country boundaries
Large cities
London Capital cities underlined

Orkney Islands
Shetland Islands
John o' Groats
Wick
Lewis
Ullapool
Inverness
Aberdeen
Hebrides
Skye
Ben Nevis ▲1342
Grampians
SCOTLAND
Mull
Oban
Dundee
Perth
Firth of Forth
Edinburgh
Islay
Glasgow
Arran
Southern Uplands
ATLANTIC OCEAN
Londonderry
NORTHERN IRELAND
Donegal Bay
L. Neagh
Belfast
Armagh
Isle of Man
Douglas
Newcastle-upon-Tyne
Carlisle
Sunderland
Middlesbrough
Pennines
IRELAND
Galway
Athlone
Dublin
Shannon
Wicklow Mts.
Wexford
Waterford
Cork
Irish Sea
Anglesey
Holyhead
Snowdon △ 1085
Cambrian Mountains
Aberystwyth
St. George's Channel
York
Bradford
Leeds
Hull
Manchester
Liverpool
Sheffield
Stoke-on-Trent
Derby
Nottingham
Trent
The Wash
UNITED KINGDOM
North Sea
NETHERLANDS
WALES
ENGLAND
Birmingham
Coventry
Leicester
Northampton
Worcester
Avon
Wye
Severn
Ouse
Norwich
Cambridge
Ipswich
Luton
Gloucester
Cotswolds
Oxford
Thames
London
Swansea
Port Talbot
Cardiff
Reading
Canterbury
Dover
Bristol
Exmoor
Southampton
Brighton
Portsmouth
Strait of Dover
Channel Tunnel
BELGIUM
Dartmoor
Bournemouth
Exeter
Isle of Wight
Plymouth
Isles of Scilly
Land's End
Penzance
English Channel
FRANCE
West from Greenwich 0° East from Greenwich

▲ **The Highlands of Scotland** are very beautiful. The hard rocks are hundreds of millions of years old, and they were eroded by glaciers in the Ice Age.

COPYRIGHT PHILIP'S

BENELUX

NETHERLANDS

AREA 41,526 sq km
POPULATION 16,491,000
MONEY Euro

BELGIUM

AREA 30,528 sq km
POPULATION 10,379,000
MONEY Euro

BENELUX is a word made up from BElgium, NEtherlands and LUXembourg. Fortunately, the first two letters of each name are the same in most languages, so everyone can understand the word. These three countries agreed to co-operate soon after World War 2. But they still have their very own King (of Belgium), Queen (of the Netherlands), and Grand Duke (of Luxembourg). They are shown in the coins (below).

The Benelux countries are all small and are the most crowded in mainland Europe, but there is plenty of countryside too. Most of the land is low and flat, so they are sometimes called the Low Countries.

▲ **Are these windmills?** Most Dutch 'windmills' are really wind-pumps. They were used to pump water up from the fields into rivers and canals. The river is higher than the land! These are at Kinderdijk, east of Rotterdam.

▲ **Bruges** is a historic town in Belgium. These old houses have survived many wars. Canals run through the town. The houses have no back door or garden – but they get a lovely view!

LUXEMBOURG

AREA 2,586 sq km
POPULATION 474,000
MONEY Euro

GAINING LAND

The map shows that a large part of the Netherlands is below sea level. For over 1000 years, the Dutch have built dykes (embankments) to keep out the sea and rivers. Then the water is pumped out. Once they used wind-pumps; today they use diesel or electric pumps. The rich farmland grows vegetables and flowers.

PUZZLE

A puzzle from the Netherlands:
● What are these yellow objects?
● What are they made of?
● Why are they for sale?
(Answers on page 96.)

WHICH COUNTRY?

These Euro coins come from the Benelux countries – but which coin belongs to which country? The text above will help you. (Answers on page 96.)

▲ **Europort, Rotterdam.** Rotterdam is by far the biggest port in the whole world. Ships come from all over the world, and barges travel along the River Rhine and the canals of Europe to reach the port. Whole families live on the barges; sometimes they even take their car with them!

Luxembourg and eastern Belgium have pleasant wooded hills called the Ardennes. Once, there was a flourishing steel industry using coal from Belgium and iron ore from Luxembourg. Today, most of the coal mines have closed and central Belgium is a problem area.

The eastern part of the Netherlands has large areas of heath and forest. But the best-known landscape is the 'polders' of the west.

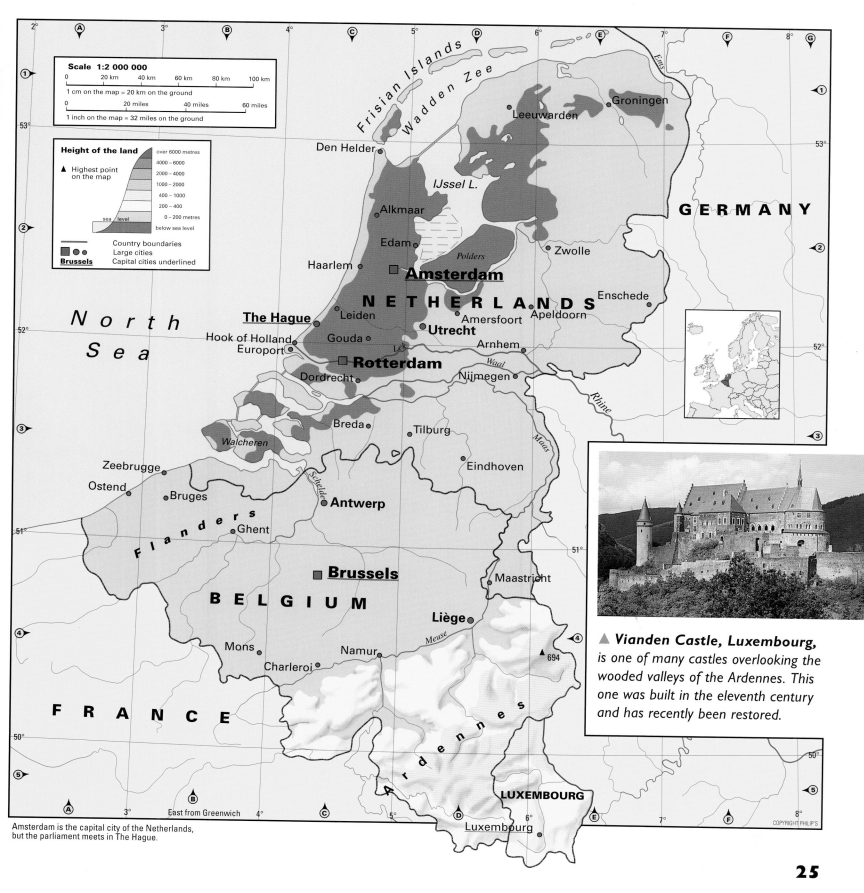

Scale 1:2 000 000

| 0 | 20 km | 40 km | 60 km | 80 km | 100 km |

1 cm on the map = 20 km on the ground

| 0 | 20 miles | 40 miles | 60 miles |

1 inch on the map = 32 miles on the ground

Height of the land

▲ Highest point on the map

	over 6000 metres
	4000 – 6000
	2000 – 4000
	1000 – 2000
	400 – 1000
	200 – 400
sea level	0 – 200 metres
	below sea level

Country boundaries
Large cities
Brussels Capital cities underlined

Frisian Islands

Wadden Zee

Ems

Groningen

Leeuwarden

Den Helder

IJssel L.

GERMANY

Alkmaar

Edam

Polders

Zwolle

Haarlem

Amsterdam

Enschede

NETHERLANDS

The Hague

Leiden

Amersfoort

Apeldoorn

Utrecht

Hook of Holland

Gouda

Lek

Europort

Arnhem

Rotterdam

Waal

Dordrecht

Nijmegen

Rhine

North Sea

Breda

Tilburg

Maas

Walcheren

Zeebrugge

Eindhoven

Ostend

Bruges

Antwerp

F l a n d e r s

Ghent

Schelde

Maastricht

Brussels

B E L G I U M

Liège

Mons

Meuse

694

Namur

Charleroi

A r d e n n e s

F R A N C E

LUXEMBOURG

Luxembourg

▲ **Vianden Castle, Luxembourg,** *is one of many castles overlooking the wooded valleys of the Ardennes. This one was built in the eleventh century and has recently been restored.*

Amsterdam is the capital city of the Netherlands, but the parliament meets in The Hague.

COPYRIGHT PHILIP'S

FRANCE

▲ *These Majorette models are made in France. They include a Renault van, a Michelin lorry, an Air France bus and a Paris bus. The most popular French cars are:*

RENAULT

CITROËN

PEUGEOT

What else can you find in your home that is made in France? In our home we have: **BIC** *ball-point pens,* **LE CREUSET** *frying-pans and saucepans,* **ARCOROC** *glassware,* **ARCOPOL** *cups, a* **MOULINEX** *mixer, and lots and lots of* **MAJORETTE** *cars!*

FRANCE is a country with three coastlines: can you see which these are? It is hot in summer in the south, but usually cool in the mountains and in the north. France is the biggest country in Western Europe, so there are big contrasts between north and south.

The highest mountains are the Alps in the south-east and the Pyrenees in the south-west. They are popular for skiing in winter and for summer holidays too. More than half the country is lowland, with wide rivers. Farming is very important: besides fruit and vegetables, France is famous for its many different cheeses and wines.

▲ **Mont Blanc.** *The 'White Mountain' is the highest mountain in Western Europe. It is 4807 metres high. Even in summer (as here) it is covered in snow. Cable-cars take tourists and skiers up the mountain, and there is a road tunnel through Mont Blanc to Italy.*

▲ **The Eiffel Tower** *was built in Paris in 1889. It was designed by Monsieur Eiffel, an engineer. It is 300 metres high and weighs 7000 tonnes! Lifts go to the top.*

FRENCH WINE

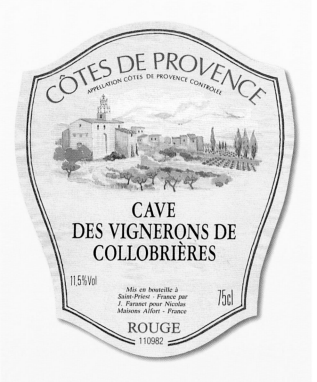

CÔTES DE PROVENCE
APPELLATION CÔTES DE PROVENCE CONTROLÉE

CAVE DES VIGNERONS DE COLLOBRIÈRES

11,5% Vol

Mis en bouteille à Saint-Priest - France par J. Faranet pour Nicolas Maisons Alfort - France

75cl

ROUGE
110982

This label is from a bottle of wine from Provence, in the south of France. It tells you where the grapes were grown and where the wine was bottled. Collobrieres is a village east of the River Rhône. The houses have red tiled roofs. Around the village are fields of fruit trees and vines. Rows of tall trees have been planted to shelter the crops from cold winds. The red grapes are picked in the autumn.

FRANCE

AREA 551,500 sq km
POPULATION 60,876,000
MONEY Euro

▲ **Market at Grasse.** *Which fruit can you recognize on this stall? (Answers on page 96.) Every town in France has a good market with fresh fruit and vegetables.*

France is changing fast. The number of people living in villages is going down, and the population of the cities is growing. People from Africa have moved here, too.

The biggest city is **Paris**, which is also the capital. Ten million people live in the Paris region. Five big new towns have been built, linked to the city centre by fast trains.

Tourists come to Paris from all over the world. Here, you can enjoy a boat trip on the River Seine past Notre Dame Cathedral, or travel east to the Disneyland Resort, Paris.

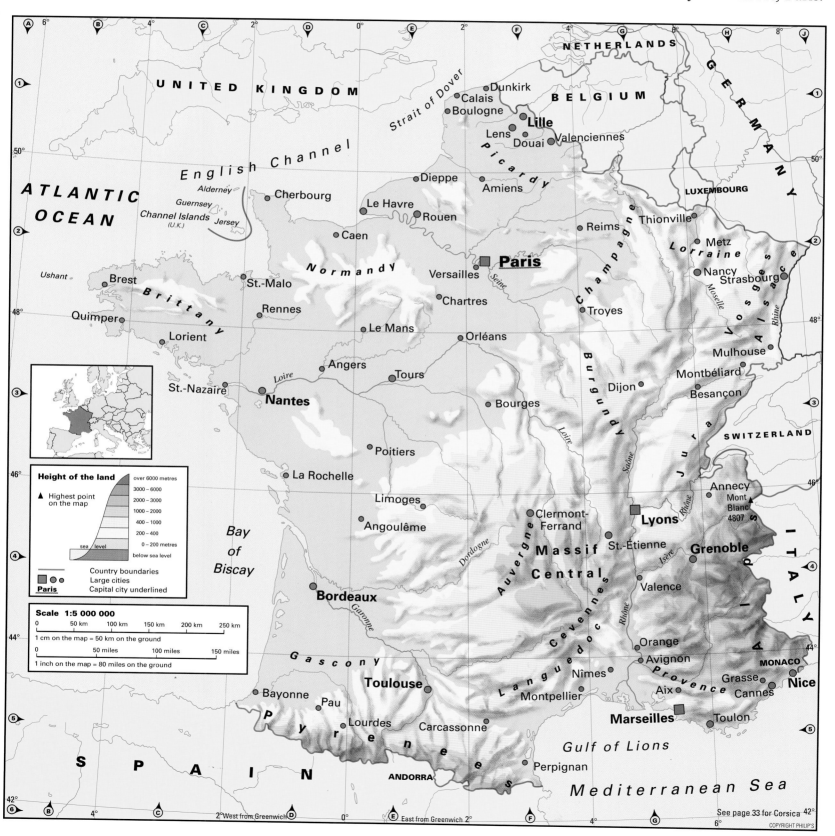

Height of the land

	over 6000 metres
	3000 – 6000
▲ Highest point on the map	2000 – 3000
	1000 – 2000
	400 – 1000
	200 – 400
	0 – 200 metres
sea level	below sea level

—— Country boundaries
■ ● ● Large cities
Paris Capital city underlined

Scale 1:5 000 000

0   50 km   100 km   150 km   200 km   250 km

1 cm on the map = 50 km on the ground

0   50 miles   100 miles   150 miles

1 inch on the map = 80 miles on the ground

See page 33 for Corsica

COPYRIGHT PHILIP'S

27

GERMANY AND AUSTRIA

GERMANY

AREA 357,022 sq km
POPULATION 82,422,000
MONEY Euro

AUSTRIA

AREA 83,859 sq km
POPULATION 8,193,000
MONEY Euro

▲ **Berlin:** *this ruined tower, next to the new tower of the Memorial Church, is left as a reminder of the destruction caused by war. It is in the city centre. Berlin is no longer divided and is once again the capital of a united Germany.*

GERMANY has more people than any other European country apart from Russia. Most of the 82 million Germans live in towns and cities. Several million people called 'guest workers' have come from southern Europe and Turkey to work in Germany's factories. But nowadays there is unemployment in Germany, as in other European countries, and many 'guest workers' have returned home. Among the many different goods made in Germany there are excellent cars: BMW, Ford, Mercedes, Opel, Porsche and Volkswagen.

There is also plenty of beautiful and uncrowded countryside. The north is mostly lowland. Parts of the south, such as the Black Forest, are mountainous and popular for holidays.

Germany was one country from 1870 to 1945. In 1990 it became one country again. From 1945 until 1990, it was divided into West Germany and East Germany, and there was a border fence between the two. In Berlin, the high wall that divided the city into east and west was knocked down in 1989.

▲ **Edelweiss** *are flowers that grow high in the Alps. They can survive in thin soil on steep slopes, and do not mind being buried by snow all winter. They are a national symbol in Austria.*

▲ **The Rhine Gorge,** *in western Germany. Castles once guarded this important river route. The River Rhine flows from Switzerland, through Germany to the Netherlands. Big barges travel between the ports and factories beside the river. Tourists travel along the river to enjoy the beautiful landscape.*

TRANSPORT

This monorail (above) is built over the River Wupper (near the River Ruhr) to save space.

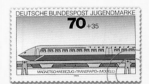

Two stamps from Germany (above) show a powerful diesel engine and a model of a 'hover-train'.

The Austrian stamp (left) shows a cable-car which takes tourists to the top of a high mountain.

AUSTRIA: Until 1918, Austria and Hungary were linked, and together ruled a great empire which included much of Central Europe and Slovenia, Croatia and Bosnia (see page 34). But now Austria is a small, peaceful country.

In the west of Austria are the high Alps, and many tourists come to enjoy the beautiful scenery and winter sports. Busy motorways and electric railways cross the Austrian Alps to link Germany with Italy.

Most Austrians live in the lower eastern part of the country. The capital, Vienna, was once at the centre of the Austrian Empire; now it is in a corner of the country.

Nine countries have borders with Germany – Austria is one of them. Try to name the others – then check your answer on the map on page 19.

▲ *Hallstatt, Austria,* is built on steep slopes which are part of the Dachstein Mountains in the eastern Alps, south-east of Salzburg. It lies beside a deep blue lake with the same name. Prehistoric remains have been found near here.

DENMARK

Baltic Sea

North Sea

Flensburg

Kiel

Rügen

Heligoland

Rostock

Lübeck

Schwerin

Bremerhaven

Hamburg

Oldenburg

Bremen

Elbe

Oder

P O L A N D

Hanover

Brunswick

Berlin

Potsdam

Bielefeld

Magdeburg

Münster

Harz Mts.

Halle

Leipzig

Essen

Dortmund

Duisburg

Ruhr

Kassel

Göttingen

Dresden

Wuppertal

Düsseldorf G E R M A N Y

Cologne

Erfurt

Gera

Neisse

Aachen

Bonn

Chemnitz

Rhine

Gorge

Ore Mts.

BELGIUM

Koblenz

Moselle

Wiesbaden

Frankfurt

Main

LUXEMBOURG

Rhine

CZECH REPUBLIC

Mannheim

Würzburg

Bohemian Forest

Heidelberg

Saarbrücken

Nuremberg

Regensburg

Danube

F R A N C E

Karlsruhe

Bavaria

Stuttgart

Black Forest

Ulm

Augsburg

Inn

Danube

Linz

Vienna

Freiburg

Danube

Salzburg

L. Constance

Munich

Hallstatt

Dachstein Mts.

LIECHTENSTEIN

Inn

Innsbruck

A U S T R I A

Graz

Tirol

Alps

▲Grossglockner
3797

Mur

HUNGARY

S W I T Z E R L A N D

Klagenfurt

I T A L Y

S L O V E N I A

NETHERLANDS

Scale 1:5 000 000

| 0 | 50 km | 100 km | 150 km | 200 km | 250 km |

1 cm on the map = 50 km on the ground

| 0 | 50 miles | 100 miles | 150 miles |

1 inch on the map = 80 miles on the ground

Height of the land

	over 6000 metres
▲ Highest point on the map	3000 – 6000
	2000 – 3000
	1000 – 2000
	400 – 1000
	200 – 400
	0 – 200 metres
sea level	below sea level

Country boundaries
Large cities
Capital cities underlined

Vienna

COPYRIGHT PHILIP'S

SPAIN AND PORTUGAL

SPAIN

AREA 497,548 sq km
POPULATION 40,398,000
MONEY Euro

PORTUGAL

AREA 88,797 sq km
POPULATION 10,606,000
MONEY Euro

SPAIN and Portugal are separated from the rest of Europe by the high Pyrenees Mountains. Most people travelling by land from the north reach Spain along the Atlantic or Mediterranean coasts.

The Meseta is the very high plateau of central Spain. Winters are very cold, and summers are very hot. The capital city, Madrid, is about 650 metres above sea level. Olives and grapes are the main crops, and both Spain and Portugal export famous wines such as sherry and port. Cars are the biggest export from Spain nowadays. Both Spain and Portugal have fine cities with great churches and cathedrals, built when they were the richest countries in the world.

▲ **Replica Columbus ship in Barcelona, Spain.** *Beyond the palm trees and the plaza (square) is a replica of the ship in which Christopher Columbus sailed across the Atlantic Ocean in 1492 to discover the 'New World' of the Americas. The voyage was paid for by the Queen of Spain.*

▲ **Portuguese fishermen** *mending their nets at Tavira, on the Algarve. They continue to land sardines and other fish, but the town relies on the tourist trade for most of its income.*

DID YOU KNOW?

Gibraltar is still a British colony, but it is only 6 square kilometres in area. Spain still owns two towns in Morocco: *Ceuta* and *Melilla*. Spain wants Gibraltar – and Morocco wants Ceuta and Melilla. The argument has been going on for nearly 300 years....

THE ALHAMBRA PALACE

The **Alhambra Palace, Granada.** This beautiful palace was built by the Moors (Arabs from North Africa). The Moors ruled southern Spain for hundreds of years, until 1492. The Arabs brought new crops and new ideas to Europe, such as oranges, rice and sugar-cane, which are still grown in Spain today.

The photo (left) of the Court of Lions shows the stone lions carved 600 years ago by Arab craftsmen.

▲ **Village in southern Spain.** *The old houses crowd closely together, and roads are very narrow: wide enough for a donkey, but not for lorries. People whitewash their houses to reflect the rays of the hot sun. Some of the roofs are used as balconies.*

People visit **Spain** for holidays: the Costa Brava (Rugged Coast), Costa Blanca (White Coast), Costa del Sol (Coast of the Sun) and the Balearic Islands.

People also enjoy holidays in the **Canary Islands**. These belong to Spain – find them on page 55. They have interesting features made by the volcanoes.

In **Portugal** the Algarve coast is the most popular holiday area. Madeira, a Portuguese island far out in the Atlantic, is another holiday area famous for its wine.

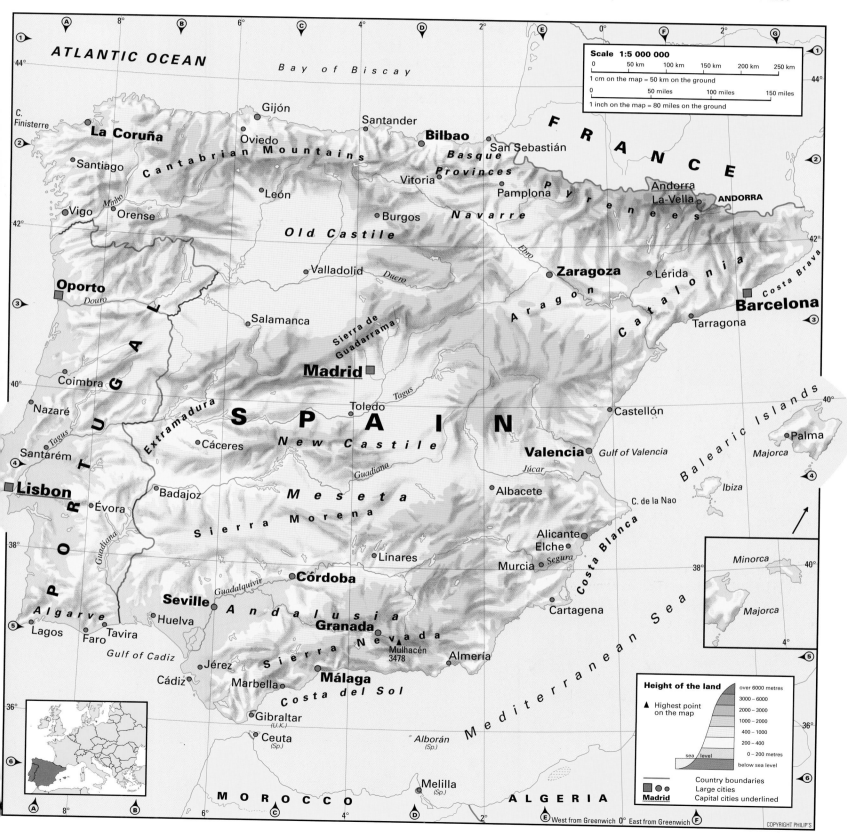

Scale 1:5 000 000

| 0 | 50 km | 100 km | 150 km | 200 km | 250 km |

1 cm on the map = 50 km on the ground

| 0 | 50 miles | 100 miles | 150 miles |

1 inch on the map = 80 miles on the ground

ATLANTIC OCEAN

Bay of Biscay

F R A N C E

C. Finisterre

La Coruña
Gijón
Santander
Bilbao
San Sebastián

Santiago
Oviedo
Cantabrian Mountains
Basque Provinces
Vitoria
Pamplona
Andorra La-Vella
ANDORRA

Vigo
Minho
Orense
León
Navarre
Pyrenees

Burgos
Old Castile
Ebro

Valladolid
Duero
Zaragoza
Lérida
Catalonia
Costa Brava

Oporto
Douro
Aragon

Salamanca
Barcelona
Tarragona

Sierra de Guadarrama

Madrid

Coimbra
Tagus

Nazaré
Toledo
Castellón
Balearic Islands

S P A I N
Palma

Santarém
Tagus
Cáceres
New Castile
Valencia
Gulf of Valencia
Majorca

Lisbon
Extremadura
Júcar
Ibiza

Évora
Badajoz
Guadiana
Meseta
Albacete
C. de la Nao

Sierra Morena
Alicante
Elche
Costa Blanca
Minorca

Guadiana
Linares
Murcia
Segura
Majorca

Córdoba
Cartagena

Seville
Guadalquivir
Andalusia

Huelva
Granada
Algarve
Sierra Nevada
Mediterranean Sea

Lagos
Faro
Tavira
Mulhacén 3478
Almería

Gulf of Cadiz
Jérez
Cádiz
Marbella
Málaga
Costa del Sol

Gibraltar (U.K.)

Ceuta (Sp.)
Alborán (Sp.)

P O R T U G A L

Melilla (Sp.)

M O R O C C O
A L G E R I A

West from Greenwich 0° East from Greenwich

Height of the land

▲ Highest point on the map

	over 6000 metres
	3000 – 6000
	2000 – 3000
	1000 – 2000
	400 – 1000
	200 – 400
sea level	0 – 200 metres
	below sea level

Country boundaries
Large cities
Madrid Capital cities underlined

COPYRIGHT PHILIP'S

31

SWITZERLAND AND ITALY

AREA 41,284 sq km
POPULATION 7,524,000
MONEY Swiss franc

▲ **The Matterhorn** in the Swiss Alps is 4478 metres high. Glaciers helped carve its shape. Zermatt is the ski resort which gives good views of the peak.

ITALY is shaped like a boot: its toe seems to be kicking Sicily! The shape is caused by the long range of fold mountains called the Apennines. The great Roman Empire was centred on Italy, and there are many Roman ruins. Yet Italy was only united as a country less than 150 years ago. Italy has lots of big factories. The Fiat car plant in Turin is one of the largest and most modern in the world.

The south of Italy and the islands of Sicily and Sardinia have hot, dry summers. These areas are much less rich than the north. Many people have moved to the north of the country to find work. But government projects are bringing factories and better roads.

In Switzerland, most people live in cities north of the Alps. Switzerland is one of the world's richest countries, with modern banks, offices and factories. Rivers, dams and waterfalls in the Alps are used for making hydro-electric power: trains, factories and homes in Switzerland all run on cheap electricity. Cable-cars powered by electricity take skiers and tourists high into the beautiful mountains. Switzerland holds some amazing world records (see below).

▲ **Venice,** in north-east Italy, is a city built in the sea. Everywhere in the old town has to be reached by boat, or on foot, because the 'roads' are canals.

ITALIAN FOOD

Large plum tomatoes are tinned (above). Many kinds of fruit are dried and used in cakes (right).

Pasta (above) is made from Italian wheat. Spaghetti, macaroni and ravioli are pastas.

SWISS RECORD BREAKERS!

- The longest road tunnel is the St Gotthard tunnel (16.32 km).
- The longest stairway is beside the Niesenbahn mountain railway, near Spiez. It has 11,674 steps!
- The steepest railway goes up Mount Pilatus. It has a gradient of 48%.
- Switzerland has been at peace with everyone since 1815. That's quite a record!

▲ **Celano, in the Abruzzo region.** This is in the Apennine Mountains in central Italy. The old hill town with its castle was a safe place to live. The new town spreads over flat land which was once a lake.

AREA 301,318 sq km
POPULATION 58,134,000
MONEY Euro

Other countries on this map:
VATICAN CITY in Rome;
SAN MARINO within Italy;
MALTA, an island country south of Italy.

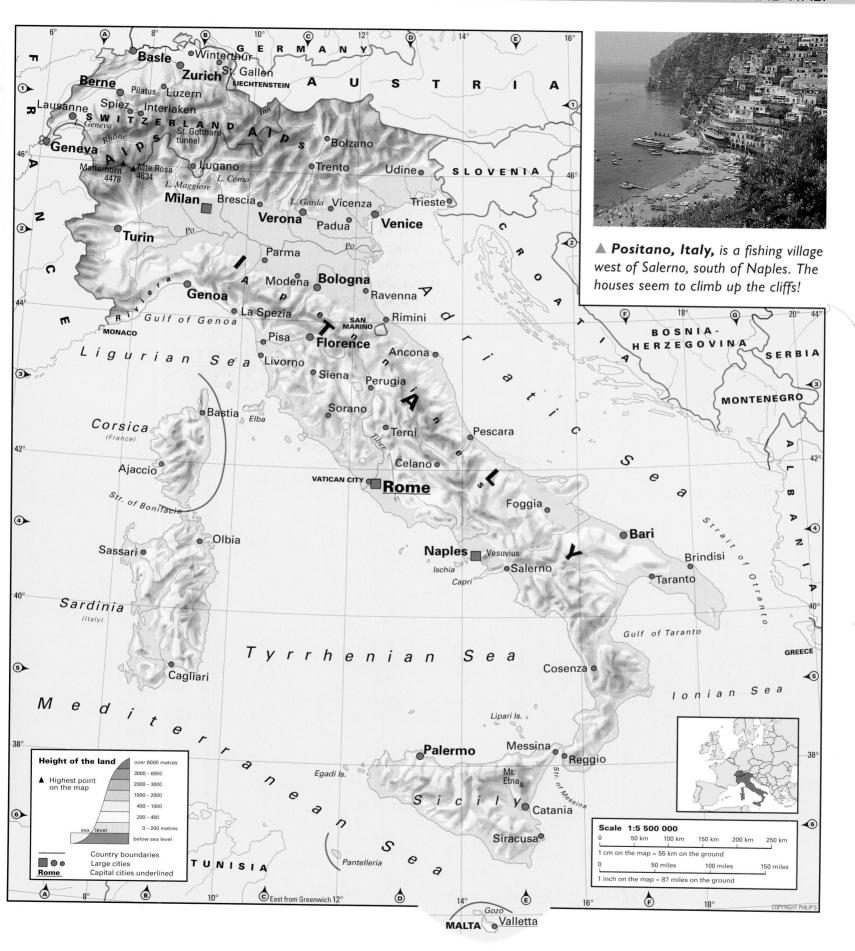

A 6° **B** 8° **C** 10° **C** 12° **D** 14° **E** 16°

FRANCE

GERMANY

Basle
Winterthur
Zurich
St. Gallen
LIECHTENSTEIN

AUSTRIA

Berne
Pilatus
Luzern
Lausanne
Spiez
Interlaken
SWITZERLAND
L. Geneva
St. Gotthard tunnel
ALPS

Geneva
Rhône
Matterhorn 4478
Mte Rosa 4634
Lugano
L. Maggiore
L. Como

Bolzano
Trento
Udine

SLOVENIA

46°

Milan
Brescia
L. Garda
Vicenza
Verona
Padua
Venice
Trieste

Turin
Po
Po

CROATIA

Parma

Genoa
Modena
Bologna
Ravenna

La Spezia
Rimini
SAN MARINO

44°

Riviera
Gulf of Genoa
Pisa
Florence
Ancona

MONACO
Livorno

Ligurian Sea
Siena
Perugia

Corsica
(France)
Bastia
Elba

Sorano

MONTENEGRO

42°

Terni
Pescara

Ajaccio
Celano

VATICAN CITY Rome

ALBANIA

Foggia

Olbia
Bari

Sassari
Naples
Vesuvius
Salerno
Brindisi

40°

Sardinia
(Italy)
Ischia
Capri
Taranto

Cagliari
Gulf of Taranto

GREECE

Tyrrhenian Sea
Cosenza

Ionian Sea

Lipari Is.

38°

Palermo
Messina
Reggio
Mt. Etna
Egadi Is.
Str. of Messina

Sicily
Catania

Siracusa

Pantelleria

TUNISIA

Mediterranean Sea

MALTA Gozo Valletta

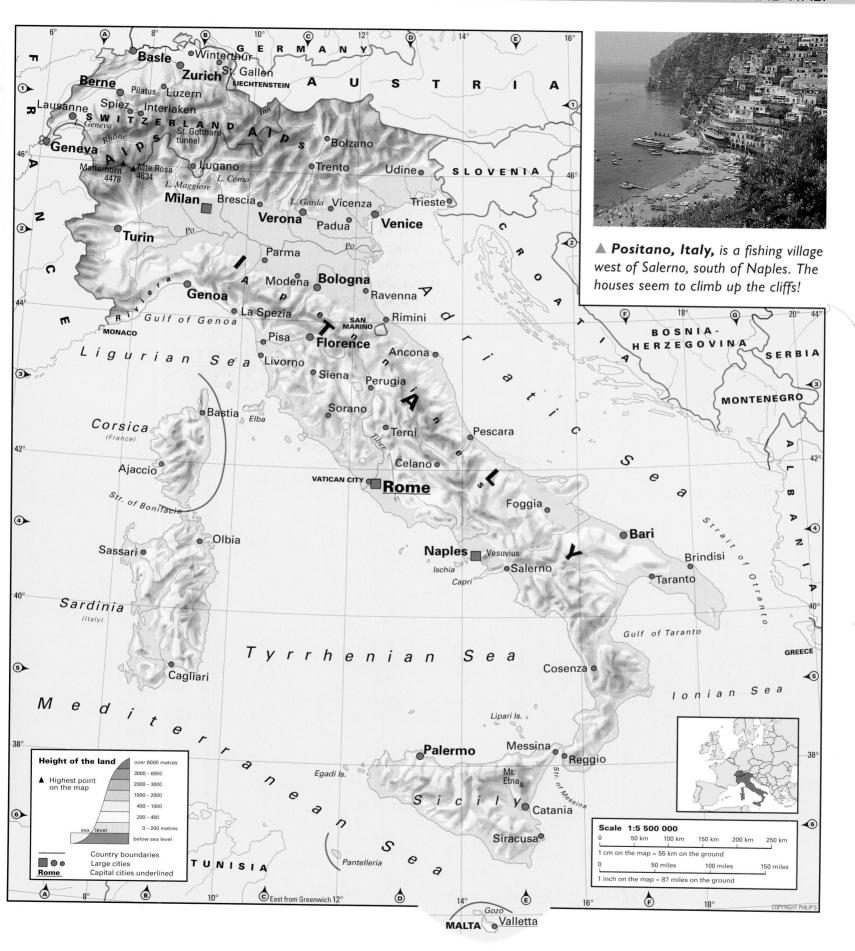

▲ Positano, Italy, is a fishing village west of Salerno, south of Naples. The houses seem to climb up the cliffs!

BOSNIA-HERZEGOVINA

SERBIA

Height of the land

over 6000 metres
▲ Highest point on the map
3000 – 6000
2000 – 3000
1000 – 2000
400 – 1000
200 – 400
0 – 200 metres
sea level
below sea level

— Country boundaries
■ ● ● Large cities
Rome Capital cities underlined

Scale 1:5 500 000

0   50 km   100 km   150 km   200 km   250 km

1 cm on the map = 55 km on the ground

0   50 miles   100 miles   150 miles

1 inch on the map = 87 miles on the ground

COPYRIGHT PHILIP'S

33

SOUTH-EAST EUROPE

GREECE

AREA 131,957 sq km
POPULATION 10,688,000
MONEY Euro

BULGARIA

AREA 110,912 sq km
POPULATION 7,385,000
MONEY Lev

ALBANIA

AREA 28,748 sq km
POPULATION 3,582,000
MONEY Lek

MOST of south-east Europe is very mountainous, except near the River Danube. Farmers keep sheep and goats in the mountains and grow grain, vines and sunflowers on the lower land.

The coastlines are popular with tourists. There are many holiday resorts beside the Adriatic Sea (**Croatia**), the Aegean Sea (**Greece** and **Turkey**), and the Black Sea (**Romania** and **Bulgaria**). The Romanians are building new ski villages in their mountains. All these countries are trying to develop new industries, but this is still one of the poorest parts of Europe.

Albania is the least-known country in all Europe: very few people visit it. No railways crossed the frontier of Albania until 1985.

Yugoslavia no longer exists. It was 1 country with 2 alphabets (Latin and Cyrillic), 3 religious groups (Roman Catholic, Orthodox and Muslim), and 4 languages. No wonder there were problems! Now there are 6 countries: **Slovenia**, **Croatia**, **Serbia**, **Montenegro**, **Bosnia-Herzegovina** and **Macedonia**.

▲ *The town of Korcula, in Croatia,* is built on an island – also called Korcula – in the Adriatic Sea, north-west of Dubrovnik. In the distance are the limestone mountains of the mainland. Until 1991, Croatia was part of Yugoslavia, but after some fighting it became independent.

THE CORINTH CANAL

A passenger liner being towed through the Corinth Canal in southern Greece. The canal was cut in 1893 and is 6.4 kilometres long. It links the Gulf of Corinth with the Aegean Sea.

THE DANUBE

This stamp shows a boat at the gorge on the River Danube called the Iron Gates, on the southern border of Romania. The Danube flows from Germany to a marshy delta beside the Black Sea.

▲ *Harvest time in Romania.* The tomato harvest is being gathered by hand on a hot summer day. The horse-drawn cart will take the full boxes back to the village for distribution.

ΑΒΓΔΕΖΗΘΙΚΛΜΝΞΟΠΡΣΤΥΦΧΨΩ
A V/B G D E Z E TH I K L M N X O P R S T Y F CH PS O

The Greek alphabet. *The Greeks developed their alphabet before the Romans, and they still use it. Some letters are the same as ours (A, B . . .), and some look the same but have a different sound (P, H . . .). The other letters are completely different. Some Greek letters appear in the Cyrillic alphabet, which is used in Bulgaria, the former Yugoslavia, and Russia (see page 41). The word 'alphabet' is formed from the first two Greek letters: alpha and beta. The Greek letter for D is called 'delta'.*

▲ **Mikonos, Greece,** *used to be a quiet village on a quiet island in the Aegean Sea. The journey from Athens was 7 hours by boat. Today, aeroplanes bring over half a million tourists to the island every year. They love the sunshine, the beaches and the boating.*

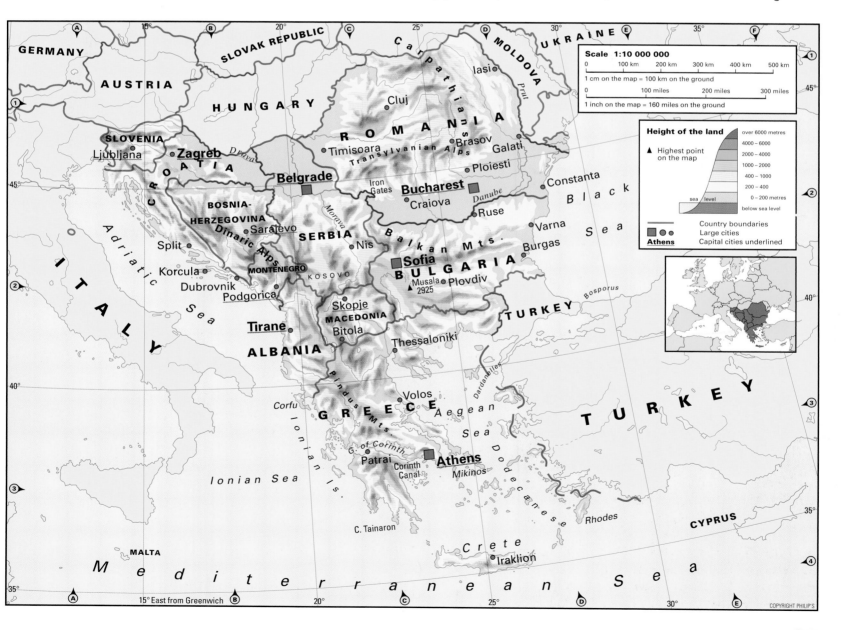

EASTERN EUROPE

POLAND

AREA 323,250 sq km
POPULATION 38,537,000
MONEY Zloty

HUNGARY

AREA 93,032 sq km
POPULATION 9,981,000
MONEY Forint

UKRAINE

AREA 603,700 sq km
POPULATION 46,711,000
MONEY Hryvnia

SEVEN countries from Eastern Europe joined the European Union in 2004: Estonia, Latvia, Lithuania, Poland, Czech Republic, Slovak Republic and Hungary.

Poland has a coastline on the Baltic Sea. There are huge shipbuilding factories at Gdansk. Towns in the south have big factories, too, where there is plenty of coal. Most of Poland is flat farmland. The magnificent mountains in the far south are being 'rediscovered' by tourists.

Czechoslovakia split into two countries in 1993. The **Czech Republic** is west of the **Slovak Republic**. Both countries have beautiful hills and mountains, with fine pine trees. Skoda cars come from the Czech Republic. Further south is **Hungary**, a small country with SEVEN neighbours – can you name them? Most of Hungary is good farmland on plains and hills.

Polish, Czech and Slovak are all Slavic languages. Hungarian is totally different: it came from central Asia. Some Hungarian speakers also live in Slovakia and Romania.

▲ **Town square in Telc, Czech Republic.** These houses date from the 1500s, when the town was rebuilt after a great fire. This is a popular place for tourists to visit. The historic centres of many towns in Eastern Europe are carefully preserved. Some have been totally rebuilt in the old style after wartime bombing.

BELARUS

AREA 207,600 sq km
POPULATION 10,293,000
MONEY Rouble

CZECH REPUBLIC

AREA 78,866 sq km
POPULATION 10,235,000
MONEY Czech koruna

SLOVAK REPUBLIC

AREA 49,012 sq km
POPULATION 5,439,000
MONEY Slovak koruna

▲ **Church in Ukraine,** where many people are Orthodox Christians. The Ukraine is Europe's biggest country, apart from Russia. The population is nearly as big as the UK or France.

▲ **Budapest, on the River Danube.** Buda and Pest were twin cities on either side of the River Danube. Now they have become Budapest, capital of Hungary. This picture shows old buildings on the hills of Buda.

▲ **The border of Poland (right) and the Slovak Republic (left)** *runs along a high ridge of the Tatra Mountains. Can you see a footpath? The steep slopes were shaped by ice.*

Six countries on this map were part of the USSR (Soviet Union) until 1991. **Estonia**, **Latvia** and **Lithuania** are called 'the Baltic republics' because they are beside the Baltic Sea. **Belarus** ('White Russia') and little **Moldova** are landlocked countries.

Ukraine is the largest country completely in Europe, but it is also one of the poorest. It has large areas of fertile farmland. Europe's largest coalfield is in the east, and there is iron ore for its steelworks.

Can you find these on the map?
- *4 seas (1 in the north; 3 in the south).*
- *A lake shared by 2 countries.*
- *A river with 4 lakes (these lakes have been made by dams).*
- *A river with a 3-letter name.*
- *A city with a 14-letter name.*
- *2 capital cities very near the sea.*
- *A mountain over 2500 metres high (the highest part of the mountain ridge in the picture, left).*
- *A peninsula that is joined to the rest of Ukraine by a very narrow piece of land.*

RUSSIA AND NEIGHBOURS

RUSSIA

AREA 17,075,400 sq km
POPULATION 142,894,000
MONEY Rouble

KAZAKHSTAN

AREA 2,724,900 sq km
POPULATION 15,233,000
MONEY Tenge

TURKMENISTAN

AREA 488,100 sq km
POPULATION 5,043,000
MONEY Manat

RUSSIA stretches across two continents, Europe and Asia. Most of the people live in the European part, west of the Ural Mountains. Some people have moved east to new towns in Siberia.

Because Russia is so huge, there are many different climates and almost all crops can be grown. The far north is snow-covered for most of the year (see page 88). Further south is the largest forest in the world – a vast area of coniferous trees stretching from the Baltic Sea to the Sea of Okhotsk in the far east. Grassy plains, called the steppes, are found south of the forest. In some parts, grain is grown on huge farms. Russia also has huge deposits of many different minerals and can supply most of the needs of its many factories.

The republics of central Asia are mostly in a desert area – hot in summer but bitterly cold in winter. With irrigation, crops such as sugar-cane and cotton grow well. Space rockets are launched from the 'Cosmodrome' in the desert of Kazakhstan.

▲ **St Basil's cathedral, Moscow,** is at one end of Red Square. It is famous for its brightly coloured domes: each one is different. In the background are the domes and towers of buildings inside the Kremlin walls. 'Kremlin' means 'fortress'. The Moscow Kremlin has a cathedral and offices of the government of Russia.

▲ **In Uzbekistan,** people still use traditional looms like this one, for weaving silk, cotton and wool – but there is modern industry as well. Uzbekistan is one of the 15 'new' countries created when the USSR broke up in 1991. Can you name them? (Page 37 will help; answers on page 96.)

THE ARAL SEA . . .

. . . is getting smaller. These ships were once in the Aral Sea, but are now on dry land. This salty lake is drying up because rivers do not refill it with enough water. The water is used to irrigate fields instead.

▲ **Siberia** has the world's largest forest. It stretches from the Ural Mountains to the far east of Russia. Most of the trees are conifers. They can survive the Siberian winters, which are long and extremely cold.

А Б В Г Д Е Ё Ж З И Й К Л М Н О П Р С Т У Ф Х Ц Ч Ш Щ Ю Я

A B V G D E YO ZH Z I Y K L M N O P R S T U F KH TS CH SH SHCH YU YA

The Cyrillic alphabet. *Russian is written in the Cyrillic alphabet. This is partly based on Latin letters (the same as English letters) and partly on Greek letters (see page 35).*

The alphabet was invented centuries ago by St Cyril, so that the Russian church could show it was separate from both the Roman and the Greek churches. In Cyrillic, R is written P, and S is written C. So the Metro is written МЕТРО.

Can you understand this message? Use the key above: **Х А Б А Р О В С К** *(square S4) is on the River* **А М У Р** *(see square S3 on the map). Now work out what the sign on the railway carriage (right) says. It is not as hard as it looks!*

Uzbekistan and some other republics of Central Asia are keeping the same language but changing their alphabet from Cyrillic to 'Latin' (as used in English and many other languages).

TRANS-SIBERIAN RAILWAY

It takes a week to cross Russia by train, and you must change your watch seven times. Here is the distance chart and timetable (only the main stops are shown).

МОСКВА–ВЛАДИВОСТОК

This is the plate on the side of the train. The translation is on page 96. This is one of the world's most exciting train journeys.

DISTANCE (IN KM)	TOWN	TIME (IN MOSCOW)	DAY
0	Moscow	15:05	1
957	Kirov	04:00	2
1818	Yekaterinburg	16:25	2
2716	Omsk	03:13	3
3343	Novosibirsk	10:44	3
4104	Krasnoyarsk	22:31	3
5184	Irkutsk	16:23	4
5647	Ulan Ude	00:02	5
6204	Chita	09:23	5
7313	Skovorodino	05:20	6
8531	Khabarovsk	01:10	7
9297	Vladivostok	13:30*	7

* This is 20:30 local time in Vladivostok.

At these stations, there is time for a quick walk – and some bartering. But don't forget to allow another week to come back!

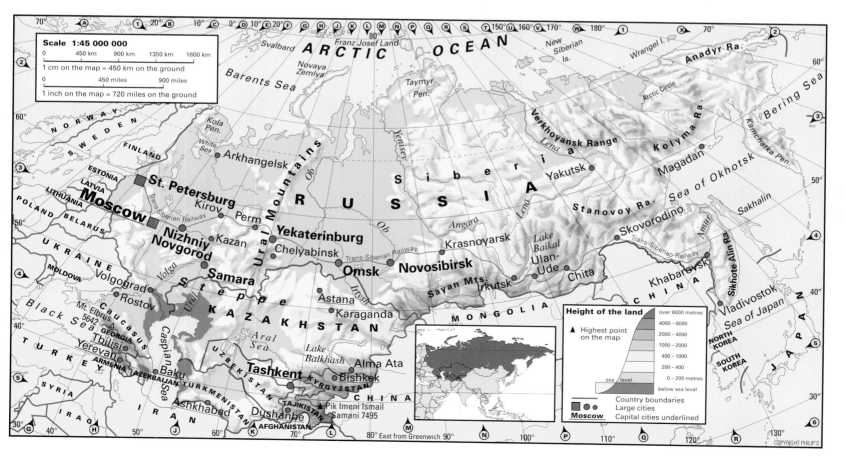

Scale 1:45 000 000

0   450 km   900 km   1350 km   1800 km
1 cm on the map = 450 km on the ground
0   450 miles   900 miles
1 inch on the map = 720 miles on the ground

Height of the land

over 6000 metres
4000 – 6000
2000 – 4000
1000 – 2000
400 – 1000
200 – 400
0 – 200 metres
below sea level

▲ Highest point on the map

Country boundaries
Large cities
Moscow Capital cities underlined

COPYRIGHT PHILIP'S

MIDDLE EAST

AREA 2,149,690 sq km
POPULATION 27,020,000
MONEY Saudi riyal

JORDAN

AREA 89,342 sq km
POPULATION 5,907,000
MONEY Jordan dinar

IRAN

AREA 1,648,195 sq km
POPULATION 68,688,000
MONEY Rial

T HE 'Middle East' is another name for 'south-west Asia'. It is the part of Asia which is closest to Europe and Africa. In fact, it is the only place where three continents meet. Turkey is partly in Europe and mostly in Asia. Of all the countries on this map, Turkey and Iran have the most people.

Most of the Middle East is semi-desert or desert. Yet many great civilizations have existed here, such as the Assyrian, the Babylonian and the Persian. Their monuments are found in the fertile valleys of the largest rivers, the Tigris and the Euphrates. During the fighting in Iraq, some historic buildings were destroyed and many people were killed.

Scarce water is used to irrigate crops in some places. In others, herds of sheep and goats are kept. Dates from Iraq come from desert oases; oranges come from irrigated land in Israel. So much water is being taken from the River Jordan that the Dead Sea is getting smaller. Some countries make fresh water from salt water, but it is expensive.

▲ *Craft stall in Istanbul. Craft industries still thrive in Turkey, and throughout the Middle East. The metal plates and pots were hammered out and decorated by hand. Europe and Asia meet at Istanbul, which used to be the capital of Turkey and was called Constantinople.*

IRAQ	STAMPS

AREA 438,317 sq km
POPULATION 26,783,000
MONEY Iraqi dinar

Progress in Qatar is shown by the highways and high-rise office blocks being built with money from oil.

HOLY CITIES OF THE MIDDLE EAST

Yemen: *an ancient multi-storey building made of mud bricks built on top of a cliff.*

Jerusalem: a Jewish boy's Bar Mitzvah ceremony at the West Wall ('Wailing Wall'). The huge stones (in the background, on the right) are all that remains of the Jewish temple. Jerusalem is a holy city for Jews, Christians and Muslims. People of all three religions live here and many pilgrims and tourists visit the city.

Mecca: crowds of pilgrims surround the Kaaba (the huge black stone, right) inside the Great Mosque. Mecca is the holiest city of Islam as it is where the prophet Mohammed was born. Muslims try to come to worship here at least once in their lifetime. But wherever they are, they face towards Mecca when they pray.

The Middle East has changed dramatically in the last 60 years. Oil was found beneath the Arabian desert and around the Persian Gulf. It is pumped out from below the desert and mountains and even from under the sea. The demand for oil has grown in Europe and all over the world. The sale of oil has made some countries very rich, especially Saudi Arabia, Kuwait and Qatar. Often the rulers have benefited most, but they have also used the money to build schools, hospitals, roads and office blocks. The 'oil boom' has meant that many foreign workers have come to these countries.

▲ **Muscat** is the capital city and chief port of Oman. The city is surrounded by rock desert and dry mountains. The Sultan has his palace here.

▲ **Camels in the desert** of the United Arab Emirates – a view that has not changed for centuries. Only camels can be kept in such dry conditions.

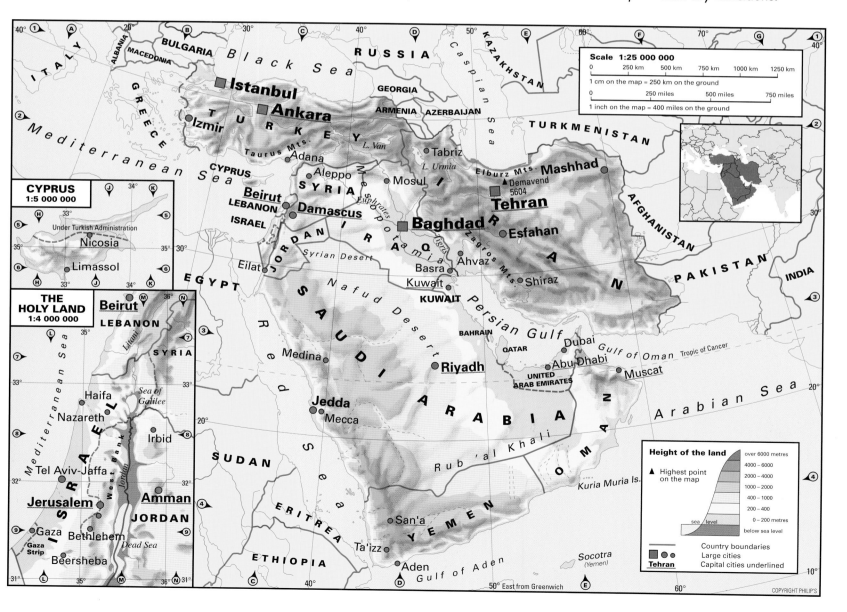

43

SOUTH ASIA

INDIA

AREA 3,287,263 sq km
POPULATION 1,095,352,000
MONEY Indian rupee
CAPITAL New Delhi

PAKISTAN

AREA 796,095 sq km
POPULATION 165,804,000
MONEY Pakistani rupee
CAPITAL Islamabad

SRI LANKA

AREA 65,610 sq km
POPULATION 20,222,000
MONEY Sri Lankan rupee

THE world's highest mountains appear on this map, including Mount Everest. The Himalayas form a great mountain chain which joins on to other high mountain areas, such as the Hindu Kush.

More than 1400 million people live in south Asia. The deserts and mountains do not have many people, but the river valleys, plains and plateaus are crowded.

Afghanistan, **Bhutan** and **Nepal** are rugged, mountainous countries.

Bangladesh is very different: it is mostly flat, low-lying land where the great rivers Ganges and Brahmaputra reach the sea.

Pakistan is a desert country, but the River Indus is used to irrigate crops.

India is the largest country. It stretches 3300 kilometres from the Himalayas to Cape Comorin. Most people live in the villages, but towns and cities are growing fast and are overcrowded. There are many modern factories, and India makes more films than any other country.

Sri Lanka (formerly called Ceylon) is a mountainous island off the coast of India.

The Maldives are a chain of low, flat, coral islands in the Indian Ocean.

▲ *Wool for carpets. This lady in northern India is winding wool which will be used to make carpets. She sits in the courtyard of her house, where the ploughs and pots and pans are also kept.*

TEA PLANTATIONS

Tea is an important crop in the hills of Sri Lanka where nights are cool, and there is plenty of rain. Women pick the new young leaves from the bushes (as shown on the stamp). The leaves are then dried

and crushed, and packed into large tea-chests for storage. 'Ceylon Tea' is one of Sri Lanka's most important exports. Where does the tea you drink come from?

INDIAN FOOD
Most Indians are vegetarians. They like hot and spicy food. How many ingredients in this picture can you name?
(*Answers on page 96.*)

AFGHANISTAN

AREA 652,090 sq km
POPULATION 31,057,000
MONEY Afghani

NEPAL

AREA 147,181 sq km
POPULATION 28,287,000
MONEY Nepalese rupee

RELIGION is very important in the lives of people in south Asia.

Hinduism is the oldest religion, and most people in India and Nepal are Hindus.

Buddhism began in India, but only Sri Lanka and Bhutan are mainly Buddhist today.

Islam is the religion of most people in Afghanistan, Pakistan and Bangladesh. There are many Muslims in India, too.

Many **Sikhs** live in northern India; there are also **Christian** groups in all these countries.

Rice is an important food crop in south Asia. It grows best where the land is flat, and where the weather is hot and wet. In a good year, rice grows in the wet fields and is ready for harvesting after four or five months. If the monsoon fails and there is a drought, the seedlings will shrivel up; too much rain and the seedlings will drown. If the rice crop fails, many people go hungry. Where irrigation is available, the farmer can control the water supply and may be able to grow two rice crops a year.

▲ *Planting rice, Kashmir, India.*
These men are planting out rice seedlings in the wet soil.

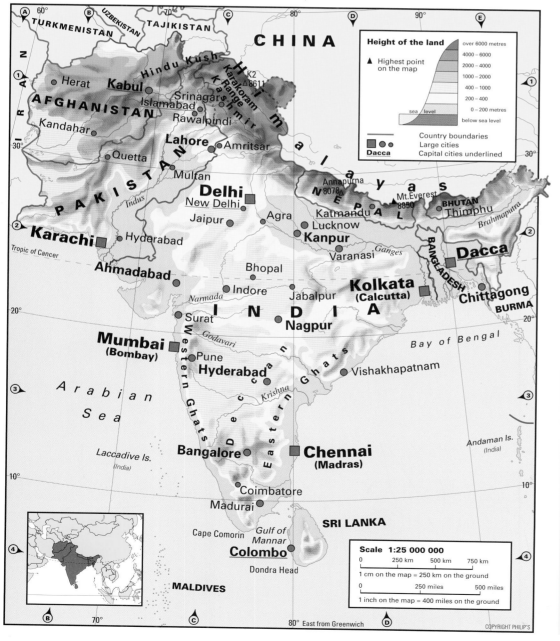

MOUNT EVEREST

Mount Everest is the world's highest mountain – 8850 metres above sea level. It was not climbed until 1953.

Everest is on the border of Nepal and Tibet (now part of China) – find it on the map in square D2. It is called 'Sagarmatha' in Nepalese, and in Chinese it is 'Qomolangma' (Queen of Mountains).

The photograph shows a glacier below the icy summit, and the bare rock that climbers have to cross. At this height, the air is very thin, so climbing is very hard and most climbers carry oxygen with them.

45

SOUTH-EAST ASIA

PHILIPPINES

AREA 300,000 sq km
POPULATION 89,469,000
MONEY Philippine peso

THAILAND

AREA 513,115 sq km
POPULATION 64,632,000
MONEY Baht

SINGAPORE

AREA 683 sq km
POPULATION 4,492,000
MONEY Singapore dollar

THE Equator crosses South-east Asia, so it is always hot. Heavy tropical rainstorms are common. The mainland and most of the islands are very mountainous.

Indonesia is the biggest country, by both area and population. It used to be called the Dutch East Indies.

The Philippines is another large group of islands, south of China. They were Spanish until 1898.

Malaysia includes part of the mainland and most of northern Borneo.

Brunei is a very small but a very rich country on the island of Borneo.

Burma (Myanmar) was part of the Indian Empire. It became independent in 1948.

Vietnam, Laos and **Cambodia** were once called French Indo-China.

Thailand has always been independent, and has a king.

▲ *Rice terraces, Bali. Rice grows on terraces cut into the mountainside in Bali. Each terrace is sown and harvested by hand. Bali is a small island east of Java. Some people claim that it is the most beautiful island of Indonesia, and in all the world!*

▲ **Singapore** *is the world's most crowded country. Old houses (in the foreground) are being pulled down and new skyscrapers are replacing them.*

GROWING RICE

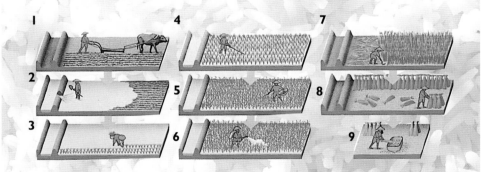

1 PLOUGHING	4 WEEDING	7 HARVESTING
2 IRRIGATION	5 FERTILIZING	8 DRYING
3 TRANSPLANTING	6 SPRAYING	9 THRESHING

Rice is the world's most important crop. The nine stages in growing rice are shown above. It is hot, hard work. Rice needs plenty of water as well as hot sunshine. New varieties of plants yield more rice, but they also need more fertilizer, more water and more care.

▲ **Floating market in Thailand.** *Farmers bring their fruit and vegetables by boat to a market at Damnoen Saduak, to the west of Bangkok. Fish are cooked on some of the boats and sold for lunch.*

The mountains of South-east Asia are covered with thick tropical forest (look at the stamp of Laos). Rare animals and plants live here. These areas are very difficult to reach and have few people. The large rivers are important routes inland. Their valleys and deltas are very crowded indeed.

Java, Bali and Singapore are among the most crowded islands in the world – yet several bigger islands, such as Sulawesi and Borneo, have very small populations.

▲ **Laos.** Elephants carry huge logs from the jungle. Laos was called Lanxang – 'land of a million elephants'.

▲ **Vietnam.** These young children are learning to draw a map of their country.

▲ **Malaysia** has a hot, wet climate. Pineapples grow well here. Some are tinned and exported.

▲ **Indonesia** is mainly an Islamic country. The moon and star (seen here above a mosque) are traditional symbols of Islam.

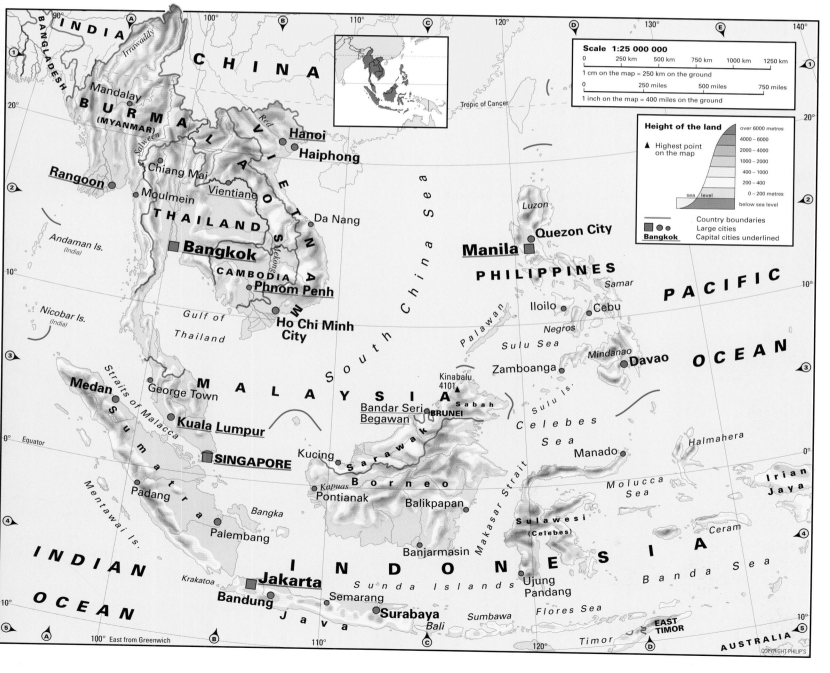

Scale 1:25 000 000

1 cm on the map = 250 km on the ground

1 inch on the map = 400 miles on the ground

Height of the land

▲ Highest point on the map

over 6000 metres
4000 – 6000
2000 – 4000
1000 – 2000
400 – 1000
200 – 400
0 – 200 metres
below sea level

Country boundaries
Large cities
Capital cities underlined

47

CHINA AND MONGOLIA

CHINA has over a billion people – more than any other country in the world. The map shows that there are many high mountains in China, such as the huge plateau of Tibet and the rugged mountains of the south-west where the Giant Pandas live. Not many people live in these mountains, nor in the deserts of the north, near Mongolia.

So the lower land of eastern China is very crowded indeed. Rice grows well south of the River Yangtze. North of the Yangtze, where the winters are colder, wheat and maize are important food crops, but it is hard to grow enough.

Taiwan is an island country which used to be called Formosa, or Nationalist China. It is not Communist and is not part of China.

Mongolia is a large desert country between Russia and China. Everywhere is more than 1000 metres above sea level. It is the emptiest country in the world, with an average of only 2 people for every square kilometre.

▲ *China's amazing mountains.* The photograph shows the amazing shapes of the limestone mountains in southern China. The mountains that look 'unreal' in Chinese paintings really are real!

▲ *Mongolia:* the Mongols were famous for their skill with bows and arrows. Today, archery is one of the main sports, along with horse-racing and wrestling.

▲ *Giant Pandas* live in the remote mountains in south-west China. Their main food is bamboo. This panda is in a special reserve because a lot of the bamboo forests have been cut down to make more farmland.

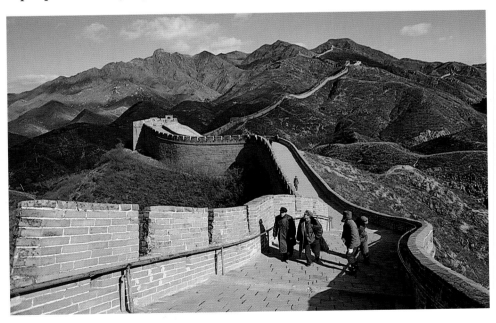

▲ *The Great Wall of China* was over 5000 kilometres long (see map) — by far the longest man-made structure in the world. Building started 2000 years ago to keep China's enemies out. This section has been repaired recently.

Mongolia has several languages and scripts. Winter is long and very cold.

CHINESE NEW YEAR

This giant dragon is being carried in the New Year procession in Hong Kong. Chinese people all over the world celebrate New Year (or Spring Festival) in February.

▲ **Shanghai** *is a large city and important port of China. Across the river from the older part of the city centre are the new skyscrapers of Pudong. On the left is the Oriental Pearl Tower.*

FACT BOX

- One out of every five people in the world is Chinese.
- The Chinese invented the compass, paper and printing.
- The Chinese have been eating with chopsticks for 3000 years!
- The place furthest from the open sea is in China: the Dzungarian Desert, which is 2400 km from the sea.
- Tibet is the highest plateau in the world. Its average height is nearly 5000 metres above sea level.

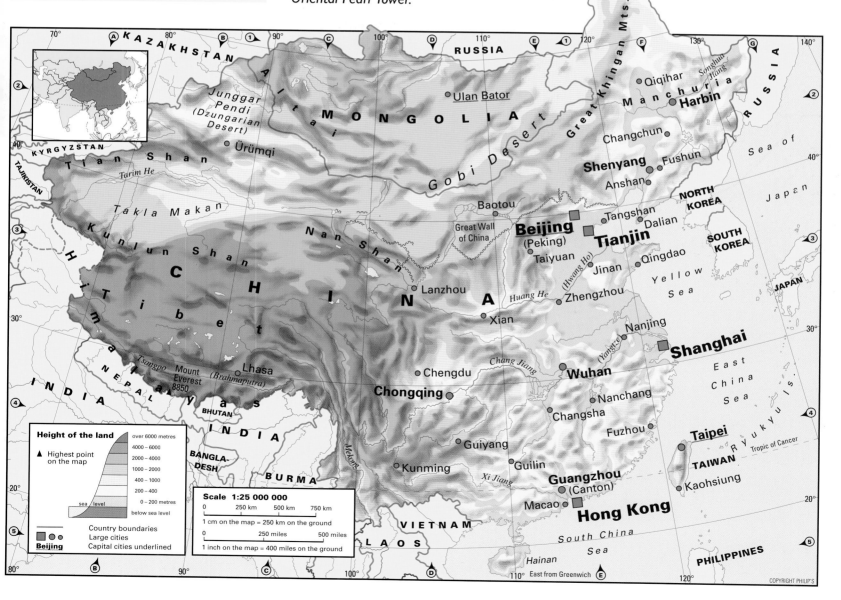

Height of the land

	over 6000 metres
	4000 – 6000
	2000 – 4000
	1000 – 2000
	400 – 1000
	200 – 400
	0 – 200 metres
	below sea level

▲ Highest point on the map

sea level

Country boundaries
Large cities
Beijing Capital cities underlined

Scale 1:25 000 000

0   250 km   500 km   750 km
1 cm on the map = 250 km on the ground

0   250 miles   500 miles
1 inch on the map = 400 miles on the ground

COPYRIGHT PHILIP'S

JAPAN AND KOREA

JAPAN

AREA 377,829 sq km
POPULATION 127,464,000
MONEY Yen
CAPITAL Tokyo
MAIN ISLAND Honshu

NORTH KOREA

AREA 120,538 sq km
POPULATION 23,113,000
MONEY North Korean won
CAPITAL Pyongyang

SOUTH KOREA

AREA 99,268 sq km
POPULATION 48,847,000
MONEY South Korean won
CAPITAL Seoul

JAPAN is quite a small country: it is smaller than France or Spain. But Japan has a big population – over twice as many people as France or Spain.

People talk of the 'Japanese miracle'. This small country is mostly mountains, has very few mines and hardly any oil, yet it has become the world's biggest producer of televisions, radios, stereo hi-fis, cameras, trucks, ships and many other things. Japanese cars and computers are admired throughout the world.

Outside the big cities, most of Japan is still beautiful and peaceful. But there are many active volcanoes.

▲ **A busy street in Kyoto.** This city was the capital of Japan for over 1000 years – until 1868. It is famous for its cooking, its gardens and shrines. High mountains surround the city on three sides.

▲ **Mount Fuji, beyond fields of tea.** Mount Fuji (Fuji-san) is Japan's most famous mountain. It is an old volcano, 3776 metres high. Tea is important in Japan. It is usually drunk as 'green tea' and often with great ceremony.

STAMP

Horyu Temple, at Nara, Japan. The beautiful temple on the right is called a pagoda. Japanese pagodas are carefully preserved. Their unusual shape originally came partly from Indian and partly from Chinese temples. The word 'Nippon' means 'Japan' in Japanese.

PUZZLE

Decorations for a Buddhist festival in South Korea.
● What are they?
● What are they made of?
(Answers on page 96.)

▲ **Bullet train.** Japan's 'bullet trains' go like a bullet from a gun! The trains run on new tracks with no sharp curves to slow them down. They provide a superb service except when there is an earthquake warning.

There are booming cities in the south of Japan, with highly skilled, hard-working people. Many of them live in the city suburbs and travel to work in overcrowded trains. Most Japanese families have small, space-saving homes. The main room is usually a living room by day, then the beds are unrolled for the night.

In southern Japan, rice is the main food crop. Some of the hillsides look like giant steps because they are terraced to make flat fields.

Korea is sandwiched between China and Japan, and has often been ruled by one or other country. Since the end of the Korean War in 1953, it has been divided into two countries by a high fence that is well guarded.

North Korea is a Communist country. It has lots of valuable minerals, but the people are poor. **South Korea** is smaller but it has a lot more people. It has become rich and exports items such as ships, electrical goods, trainers and jeans.

▲ **South Korea.** *Seoul has been the capital of Korea since 1392 – but is now only the capital of South Korea. These children are playing on one of the many hills in the city.*

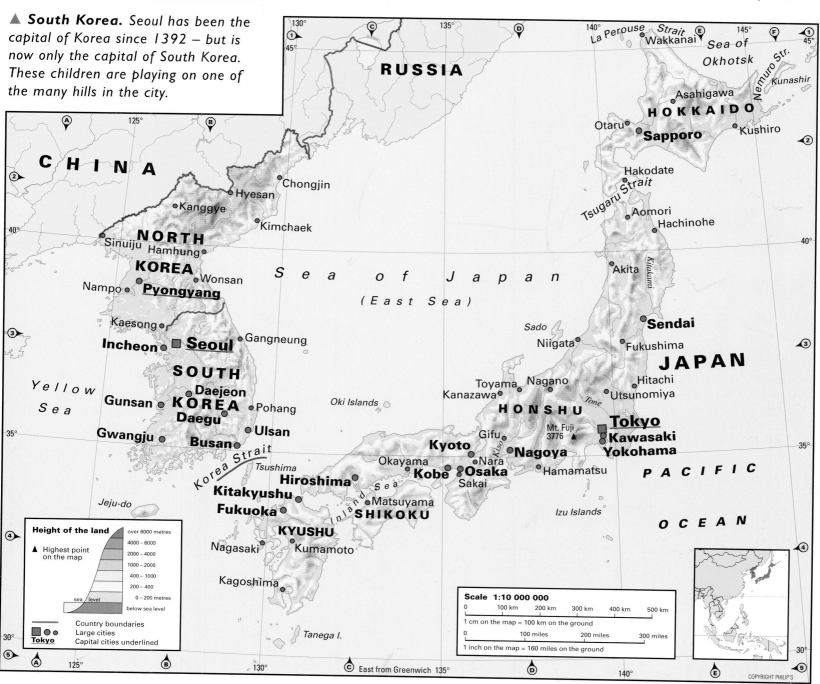

Scale 1:10 000 000

0   100 km   200 km   300 km   400 km   500 km

1 cm on the map = 100 km on the ground

0   100 miles   200 miles   300 miles

1 inch on the map = 160 miles on the ground

Height of the land
- over 6000 metres
- 4000 – 6000
- 2000 – 4000
- 1000 – 2000
- 400 – 1000
- 200 – 400
- 0 – 200 metres
- below sea level

▲ Highest point on the map

sea level

Country boundaries
Large cities
Tokyo Capital cities underlined

COPYRIGHT PHILIP'S

51

AFRICA

MOST of the countries of Africa have quite small populations – except for Nigeria and Egypt. But everywhere the population is growing fast. It is difficult to provide enough schools and clinics for all the children and there are not enough good jobs.

Imagine travelling southwards across Africa, along the 20°E line of longitude. You start in Libya. Your first 1000 kilometres will be across the great Sahara Desert (where you must travel in winter) – sand, rock and the high rugged Tibesti Mountains. Then you reach thorn bushes, in the semi-desert Sahel area of Chad.

By 15°N you are into savanna – very long grass and scattered trees. You cross the country known as CAR for short. The land becomes greener and at about 5°N you

reach the equatorial rainforest . . . a real jungle! You are now in Congo.

Then the same story happens in reverse – savanna in Angola; then semi-desert (the Kalahari and the Karoo). Now you come down to green fields, fruit trees and vines that grown in the far south. Finally, you reach the coast at the Cape of Good Hope – a journey of nearly 8000 kilometres.

▲ **Railways** are vital for exports from Africa – especially for the 'landlocked' countries.

▲ **Children in Ghana.** Everywhere in Africa, there are lots of children. The fathers of these children are fishermen: in the background you can see nets drying and big dug-out canoes. The canoes are made from the huge trees of the rainforest, and can cope with big waves in the Gulf of Guinea.

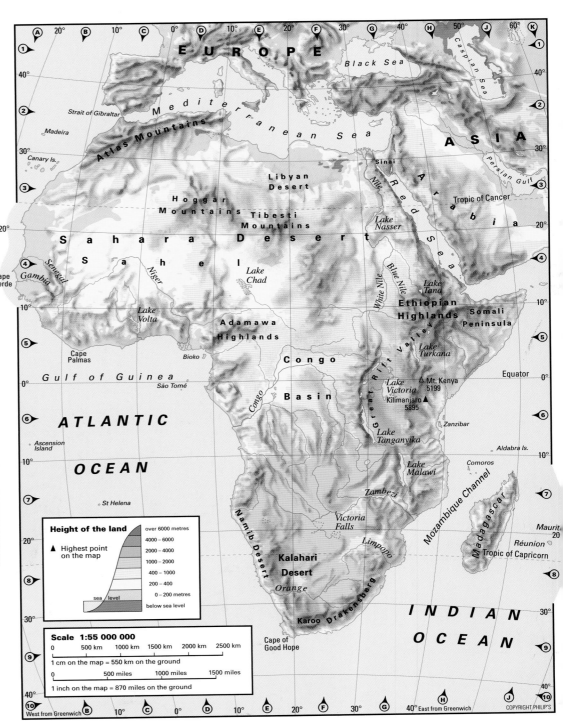

Height of the land

▲ Highest point on the map

over 6000 metres
4000 – 6000
2000 – 4000
1000 – 2000
400 – 1000
200 – 400
0 – 200 metres
sea level
below sea level

Scale 1:55 000 000

0   500 km   1000 km   1500 km   2000 km   2500 km

1 cm on the map = 550 km on the ground

0   500 miles   1000 miles   1500 miles

1 inch on the map = 870 miles on the ground

COPYRIGHT PHILIP'S

ORIGIN OF COUNTRY NAMES

CHAD Named from Lake Chad
GAMBIA, NIGER, NIGERIA From big rivers
GHANA, BENIN, MALI Names of great
  empires in West Africa a long time ago
IVORY COAST Ivory, from the tusks of
  elephants, was traded along this coast
NAMIBIA From the Namib Desert
SIERRA LEONE 'Lion Mountain'
(Portuguese)
TANZANIA From *Tanganyika* (the
  mainland) and the island of *Zanzibar*

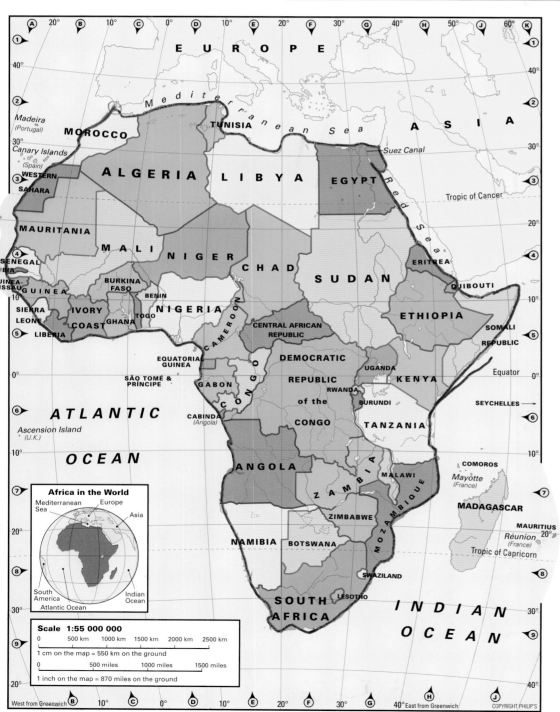

▲ **The pyramids of Egypt** *are tombs built by slaves over 4500 years ago. The picture shows the largest, which are at Giza, near Cairo. They are still the largest buildings in the whole of Africa. They are near the River Nile, in the Sahara Desert.*

COINS OF AFRICA

All the 55 countries of Africa have their own banknotes and stamps. Most countries have coins as well. Pictures on the coins usually show something about the country. The 5 Bututs coin from The Gambia (above) shows a fine sailing ship. There is Arabic writing because many people are Muslims. The 10 Kobo coin from Nigeria shows palm trees.

AFRICAN FACTS

AREA 30,319,000 sq km
HIGHEST POINT Mount Kilimanjaro
  (Tanzania), 5895 metres
LOWEST POINT Shores of Lake Assal
  (Djibouti), 155 metres below sea level
LONGEST RIVER Nile, 6800 km
  (also a world record)
LARGEST LAKE Lake Victoria
  (East Africa), 69,484 sq km
BIGGEST COUNTRY Sudan, 2,505,813 sq km
SMALLEST COUNTRIES
  Mainland: Gambia, 11,295 sq km;
  Islands: Seychelles, 455 sq km (see page 9)

Scale 1:55 000 000
1 cm on the map = 550 km on the ground
1 inch on the map = 870 miles on the ground

53

NORTH AFRICA

EGYPT

AREA 1,001,449 sq km
POPULATION 78,887,000
MONEY Egyptian pound

MOROCCO

AREA 446,550 sq km
POPULATION 33,241,000
MONEY Moroccan dirham

MALI

AREA 1,240,192 sq km
POPULATION 11,717,000
MONEY CFA franc

MOST of North Africa is desert – but not all. The coastlines and mountains of north-west Africa get winter rain: good crops are grown and the coasts of Tunisia and Morocco are popular with tourists.

All these countries are Islamic. Morocco has the oldest university in the world: the Islamic University in Fez. The largest country in Africa is the Sudan. A civil war has continued for years because the people of the far south do not want to be ruled by the Islamic north.

People can live in the desert if there is water. Some modern settlements have been built deep in the desert where there are valuable minerals, and water is pumped from underground. These minerals are the main reason why some countries are richer than others. Algeria and Libya have plenty of oil beneath the desert.

South of the Sahara is the 'Sahel' – a large semi-desert area. Some years have good rains; some years very little rain. Mali, Niger and Chad are among the poorest nations in the world.

▲ *A market near Timbuktu, in Mali,* is a place to meet as well as to trade. People bring the goods they hope to sell in locally made baskets or in re-used cartons which they balance on their heads.

SUDAN

AREA 2,505,813 sq km
POPULATION 41,236,000
MONEY Sudanese dinar

SUEZ CANAL

This old print shows the procession of ships through the Suez Canal at its opening in December 1869. The canal links the Mediterranean with the Red Sea (see map: G1). It was dug in 1859–69 by Arabs, organized by a Frenchman, Ferdinand de Lesseps. Before the canal opened, the route by sea from Europe to India and the Far East was around the whole of Africa.

▲ *Oasis near Lake Djerid, Tunisia.* Water is just below the ground, so date palms can grow well. But in the background, great sand dunes loom on the skyline. If they advance, they may cover the oasis and kill the crops.

▲ *Mosque in Morocco.* This tower is a minaret: part of an Islamic mosque. It is used to announce the times of prayer to all the village. The village is in the Ziz River valley, south of the Atlas Mountains of Morocco. Notice the flat roofs of the houses and the date palms.

Egypt is a desert country; its fertile land is 'the gift of the River Nile'. It has the biggest population of any North African country. Its capital, Cairo, is one of the biggest cities in the world. The River Nile brings water to the valley and delta. The land is carefully farmed (with irrigation) and crowded with people; the rest of Egypt is almost empty. The world population map on page 11 makes the contrast very clear. The map below shows that part of the desert is below sea level.

The lack of rain has helped to preserve many of the monuments, palaces and tombs built by the ancient Egyptians. The pyramids at Giza, near Cairo, are about 4500 years old (page 53). They are the only one of the Seven Wonders of the ancient world still surviving.

THE SAHARA DESERT

The Sahara is the biggest desert in the world. It is over 9 million sq km in size. From west to east it is over 5000 km; from north to south it extends about 2000 km and it is still growing.

THE HOTTEST SHADE TEMPERATURE ever recorded, 58°C, was in Al Aziziyah, Libya, in 1922.

THE SUNNIEST PLACE in the world, over 4300 hours of sunshine per year, is in the eastern Sahara.

THE HIGHEST SAND DUNES in the world, 430 metres high, are in central Algeria (see below).

THE LONGEST RIVER in the world is the River Nile, 6800 km long.

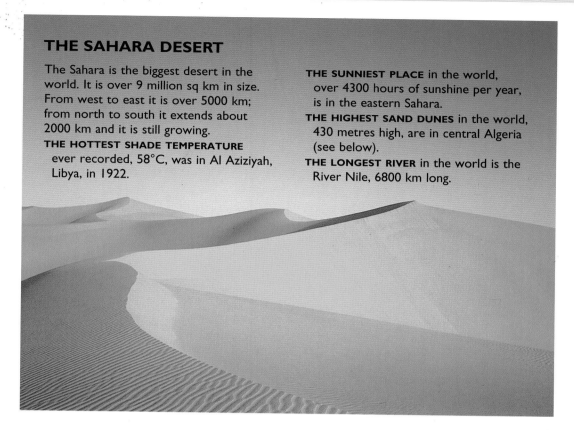

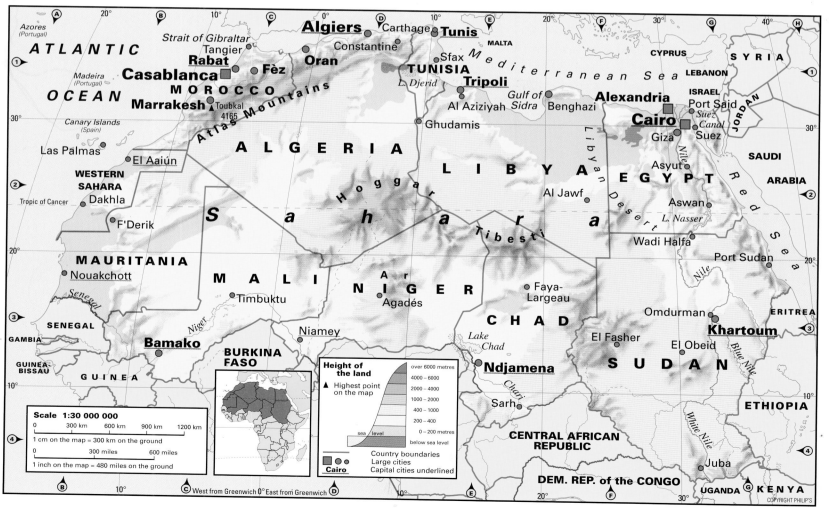

Scale 1:30 000 000

0   300 km   600 km   900 km   1200 km

1 cm on the map = 300 km on the ground

0   300 miles   600 miles

1 inch on the map = 480 miles on the ground

Height of the land
▲ Highest point on the map

over 6000 metres
4000 – 6000
2000 – 4000
1000 – 2000
400 – 1000
200 – 400
0 – 200 metres
sea level
below sea level

Country boundaries
Large cities
Capital cities underlined

COPYRIGHT PHILIP'S

WEST AFRICA

NIGERIA

AREA 923,768 sq km
POPULATION 131,860,000
MONEY Naira

THE GAMBIA

AREA 11,295 sq km
POPULATION 1,642,000
MONEY Dalasi

IVORY COAST

AREA 322,463 sq km
POPULATION 17,655,000
MONEY CFA franc

THERE are lots of countries in West Africa. In the last 300 years, European countries grabbed parts of the coastline and later they took over the inland areas as well. Now, all the countries are independent, but still use the language of those who once ruled them. English, French, Spanish or Portuguese is spoken. Many Africans speak a European language as well as one or more African languages.

Nigeria is the largest and most important country in West Africa. It has over 131 million people – more than any other African country. About half the people are Muslims, the other half are mainly Christians. Although English is the official language, there are about 240 other languages in Nigeria!

In many parts of West Africa, there is rapid progress. Most children now go to primary school, and the main cities have television and airports. But many people are still very poor. Civil war has made poverty much worse in some countries – for example, in Sierra Leone and Liberia.

▲ **Village in Cameroon:** *building houses with mud for the walls and tall grass for thatch. These materials are free and the homes are less hot than those with corrugated iron roofs.*

LIBERIA

AREA 111,369 sq km
POPULATION 3,042,000
MONEY Liberian dollar

▲ **Women pounding yams, Benin.** *They use a large wooden bowl and long pestles (pounding sticks) to break up and mash the yams. These root crops are eaten at most meals. It is very hard work: much easier if it is shared! They are probably singing to help keep a rhythm for using the pestles. The baby will love this!*

TWO TYPES OF OIL

Nigeria pumps up lots of oil from under the Niger delta. Oil has brought money to some people, but pollution to others.

8k NIGERIA OIL INDUSTRY

2b AGRICULTURE
OIL PALM
The Gambia

Palm oil comes from oil-palm trees. They grow well where it is hot and wet all year. The trees are planted in rows in a plantation. You can see the fruit hanging from the trees. The photograph on the next page shows the harvested fruit.

▲ **Market day, Nigeria.** *Red peppers for sale in Benin City, in southern Nigeria. Red peppers are very popular in West Africa – they give a strong flavour in cooking. Markets are important in both towns and villages throughout Africa.*

The southern part of West Africa, near the Equator, is forested. The tall trees are being felled for their hardwood. Many crops are grown in the forest area and sold overseas: cocoa (for chocolate-making); coffee, pineapples and bananas; rubber (for car and lorry tyres). The main food crops are root crops, such as cassava and yams.

Further north, the trees thin out and there is savanna. The tall grass with some trees is suitable for cattle farming. There are big herds of cattle, and beautiful leather goods are on sale in the markets. Cotton and groundnuts (peanuts) are grown in the savanna lands. The main food crops are grass-like: rice, maize and millet. In the far north of West Africa there is semi-desert: the Sahara is advancing southwards, and Lake Chad has shrunk in size.

▲ *Palm-oil harvest, Ghana. These people are carrying heavy baskets full of oil-palm fruit. The oil palm grows in the hot, wet climate of the tropical forest. The fruits grow in bunches, with as many as 3000 bright-red palm fruits in a bunch. The fruit and the kernels are crushed in a factory to obtain oils. These oils are very useful for cooking and in making soap.*

▲ *Yeji ferry, Ghana. This big ferry carries lorries, cars, people and their heavy loads across Lake Volta. This man-made lake flooded Ghana's main road to the north. As the water rose in the new lake, the trees and much of the wildlife died. A fifteenth of all Ghana's land was 'lost' under the lake, and new villages had to be built.*

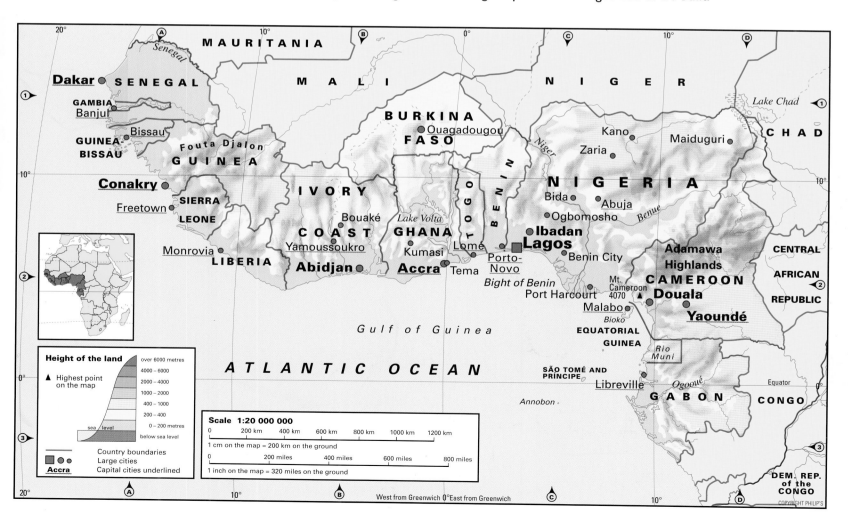

Scale 1:20 000 000

1 cm on the map = 200 km on the ground

1 inch on the map = 320 miles on the ground

Height of the land
over 6000 metres
4000 – 6000
2000 – 4000
1000 – 2000
400 – 1000
200 – 400
0 – 200 metres
below sea level
▲ Highest point on the map
sea level

Country boundaries
Large cities
Capital cities underlined

CENTRAL AND EAST AFRICA

KENYA

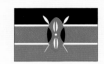

AREA 580,367 sq km
POPULATION 34,708,000
MONEY Kenyan shilling

ETHIOPIA

AREA 1,104,300 sq km
POPULATION 74,778,000
MONEY Birr

CONGO (DEM. REP.)

AREA 2,344,858 sq km
POPULATION 62,661,000
MONEY Congolese franc

CENTRAL Africa is mostly lowland, with magnificent trees in the equatorial rainforest near the River Congo. Some timber is used for buildings and canoes (see photograph right); some is exported. The cleared land can grow many tropical crops.

East Africa is mostly high savanna land with long grass, and scattered trees. Some parts are reserved for wild animals; in other parts, there are large farms for export crops such as coffee and tea. But in most of East Africa, the people keep cattle and grow crops for their own needs.

The Somali Republic, Djibouti and Eritrea are desert areas, but the mountain areas of Ethiopia get plenty of rain. There have been terrible wars in Ethiopia, Eritrea and Somalia. Wars have made the famines even worse.

In 1994 and 1995, a civil war in Rwanda led to a million deaths and more than a million refugees travelling to Congo and Tanzania. Wars like this damage people, the animals and the environment. The United Nations tries to stop wars *before* they start.

▲ *The River Congo at Mbandaka.* Children who live near the river learn to paddle a dug-out canoe from an early age. The boats are hollowed out of a single tree with an axe. The River Congo is an important transport route. Mbandaka is a river port about four days by steamer from Kinshasa.

FARMING IN EAST AFRICA

Sisal is a useful crop – you can see the fibre drying in the sun. It will be used to make string, rope and sacks.

Tea will grow in the cooler mountains. The leaves are picked by hand. It is hard work in hot sunshine.

▲ *In a game reserve in Kenya,* a group of Grevy's Zebra graze the savanna grassland. In the dry season, the grass is brown, but in the rainy season it is tall and green. The game reserves are carefully managed and people come from all over the world to see the wildlife.

▲ *Gorillas in Rwanda.* These gorillas live high up in the forested mountains. They are at risk as the trees are being cut down.

▲ *Buses in the centre of Nairobi, Kenya.* This modern capital city has many high-rise buildings – yet only 100 years ago there was no town here.

In all these countries, there are many signs of development: new farm projects, new ports and roads, new clinics and schools. But there is much poverty, too, and people are moving to the cities.

The population of this area is growing fast. It has doubled in less than 25 years. Some of these countries have the world's highest population growth rates, and more than half the population is young.

▲ *Mount Kilimanjaro, Tanzania. Africa's highest mountain is the beautiful cone of an old volcano. It is near the Equator, but high enough to have snow all year.*

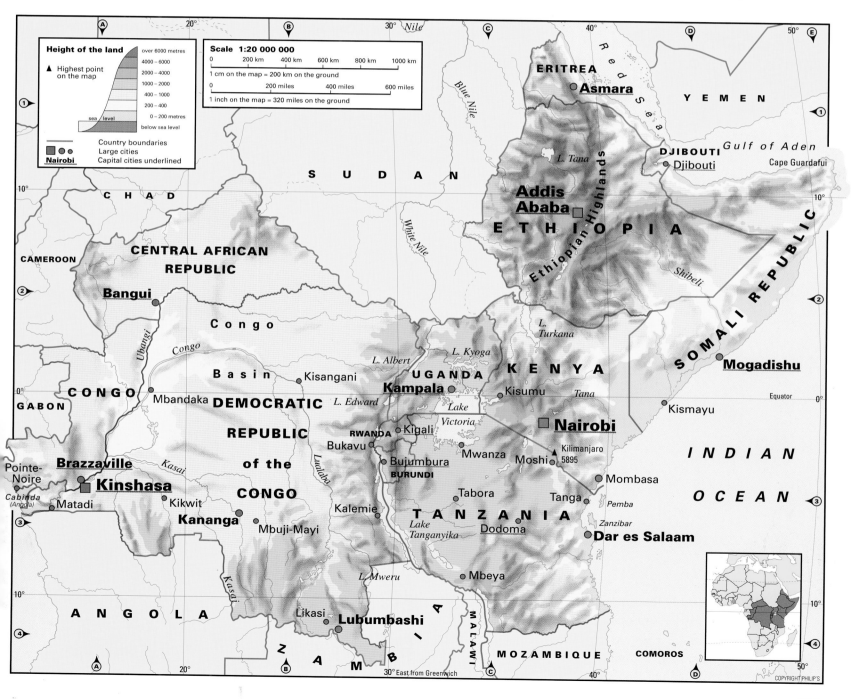

Height of the land

	over 6000 metres
	4000 – 6000
	2000 – 4000
	1000 – 2000
	400 – 1000
	200 – 400
	0 – 200 metres
	below sea level

▲ Highest point on the map

sea level

Country boundaries
Large cities
Nairobi Capital cities underlined

Scale 1:20 000 000

0	200 km	400 km	600 km	800 km	1000 km

1 cm on the map = 200 km on the ground

0	200 miles	400 miles	600 miles

1 inch on the map = 320 miles on the ground

ERITREA
● **Asmara**
YEMEN

Red Sea

Blue Nile

DJIBOUTI
● Djibouti

Gulf of Aden

Cape Guardafui

S U D A N

L. Tana

CHAD

Addis Ababa ☐

E T H I O P I A

Ethiopian Highlands

Shibeli

CAMEROON

CENTRAL AFRICAN REPUBLIC

C o n g o

White Nile

SOMALI REPUBLIC

● **Bangui**

Ubangi

Congo

B a s i n

● Kisangani

L. Turkana

● **Mogadishu**

C O N G O

Mbandaka ●

DEMOCRATIC

L. Albert

L. Kyoga

UGANDA

Kampala ●

K E N Y A

● Kisumu

Tana

GABON

L. Edward

Lake

● Kismayu

Equator

REPUBLIC

RWANDA

● **Kigali**

Victoria

☐ **Nairobi**

Bukavu ●

I N D I A N

Pointe-Noire

Brazzaville

Kasai

of the

● **Bujumbura**

Mwanza ●

Moshi ● ▲ Kilimanjaro 5895

● Mombasa

O C E A N

Cabinda (Angola)

☐ **Kinshasa**

Lualaba

BURUNDI

● Matadi

CONGO

T A N Z A N I A

Tabora ●

Tanga ●

Pemba

● Kikwit

Kananga

Kasai

● Mbuji-Mayi

Kalemie ●

Lake Tanganyika

Dodoma

Zanzibar

● **Dar es Salaam**

L. Mweru

● Mbeya

A N G O L A

● Likasi

Lubumbashi ●

Z A M B I A

M A L A W I

M O Z A M B I Q U E

COMOROS

30° East from Greenwich

COPYRIGHT PHILIP'S

SOUTHERN AFRICA

ANGOLA

AREA 1,246,700 sq km
POPULATION 12,127,000
MONEY Kwanza

ZAMBIA

AREA 752,618 sq km
POPULATION 11,502,000
MONEY Kwacha

SOUTH AFRICA

AREA 1,221,037 sq km
POPULATION 44,188,000
MONEY Rand

MOST of southern Africa is a high, flat plateau. The rivers cannot be used by ships because of big waterfalls like the Victoria Falls (see photograph right). But the rivers can be useful. Two huge dams have been built on the River Zambezi – at Kariba (in Zambia) and at Cabora Bassa (in Mozambique). The map shows the lakes behind each dam. The power of the falling water is used to make electricity.

Angola and Mozambique used to be Portuguese colonies, and Portuguese is still their official language – though many different African languages are spoken, too. Most of the other countries shown on the map have English as their official language.

The map shows you that many southern African countries are landlocked: they have no coastline, so it is more expensive to export their products. The railways leading to the ports in neighbouring countries are very important. Copper from **Zambia** and **Botswana** is sent abroad in this way.

▲ **The Victoria Falls** are on the River Zambezi, at the border of Zambia and Zimbabwe. Africans call the falls Mosi-oi-tunya – 'the smoke that thunders'. They were named after the English Queen Victoria by the explorer David Livingstone. The falls are more than a kilometre wide and over 100 metres high. The dense forest in the foreground relies on the spray from the falls.

MOZAMBIQUE

AREA 801,590 sq km
POPULATION 19,687,000
MONEY Metical

▲ **Cape Town, South Africa.** The flat-topped mountain is called 'Table Mountain'. It looks as flat as a table. When cloud covers it, it is called 'the tablecloth'! Cape Town is near the Cape of Good Hope, the most southerly point in Africa.

A VILLAGE IN ZAMBIA

A Zambian girl drew this picture of her village during a lesson at her school. Her village is close to the River Zambezi in the west of Zambia. Look for a well, a man hoeing, a fisherman and a man looking after cattle. On the road there is a bus, a car and a van.

▲ **Ring-tailed Lemur, Madagascar.** The island of Madagascar has wonderful forests and some of its wildlife is unique. But several species are under threat of extinction.

The **Republic of South Africa** is the wealthiest country in Africa. The world's largest diamond was found here. It has the world's richest gold mine and the world's deepest mine. People rushed to the area around Johannesburg when gold was found in the 1880s. Now it is South Africa's largest city.

Most of the people are still very poor. For many years, black people were kept apart from the rich white people who used to rule the country. In 1994 they gained the vote and now they govern the country.

Namibia and **Botswana** are dry areas, with small numbers of people. Some of the rivers in this area never reach the sea. The map on this page shows big swamps and 'salt pans': these are the places where the river water evaporates.

Lesotho is a small mountainous country, completely surrounded by the Republic of South Africa.

Madagascar is the fourth largest island in the world. The people and their language are a mixture of African and Indonesian. Its forests are home to very rare animals.

▲ *Children in Mozambique* hope *for a better future after many years of war. Their country is one of the poorest in Africa, and has also suffered from disastrous floods and drought.*

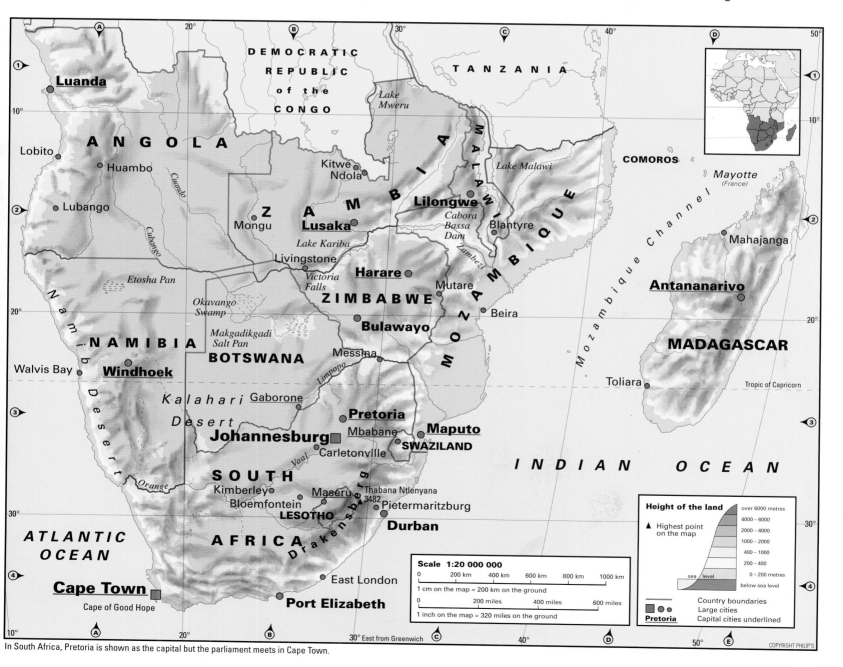

Scale 1:20 000 000

1 cm on the map = 200 km on the ground

1 inch on the map = 320 miles on the ground

Height of the land

over 6000 metres
4000 – 6000
2000 – 4000
1000 – 2000
400 – 1000
200 – 400
0 – 200 metres
below sea level

▲ Highest point on the map
sea level

Country boundaries
Large cities
Pretoria Capital cities underlined

In South Africa, Pretoria is shown as the capital but the parliament meets in Cape Town.

COPYRIGHT PHILIP'S

THE PACIFIC

◄ **This stamp from Fiji** shows one of the 300 islands that are part of this country. This is a low coral island with white sand beaches and coconut palms.

THIS map shows half the world. Guess which place is furthest from a continent: it is to be found somewhere in the south Pacific. The Pacific Ocean also includes the deepest place in the world: the Mariana Trench (11,022 metres deep). It would take over an hour for a steel ball weighing half a kilogram to fall to the bottom!

There are thousands of islands in the Pacific. Some are volcanic mountains, while many others are low, flat coral islands. Coral also grows around the volcanoes.

A few islands have valuable minerals – for example Bougainville (copper) and Nauru (phosphates). But some islands will disappear if the sea level rises.

▲ **Coral reef in French Polynesia,** from the air. Coral BELOW sea level is ALIVE! A reef is built up from the shells of dead coral. Gradually plants colonize parts of the reef.

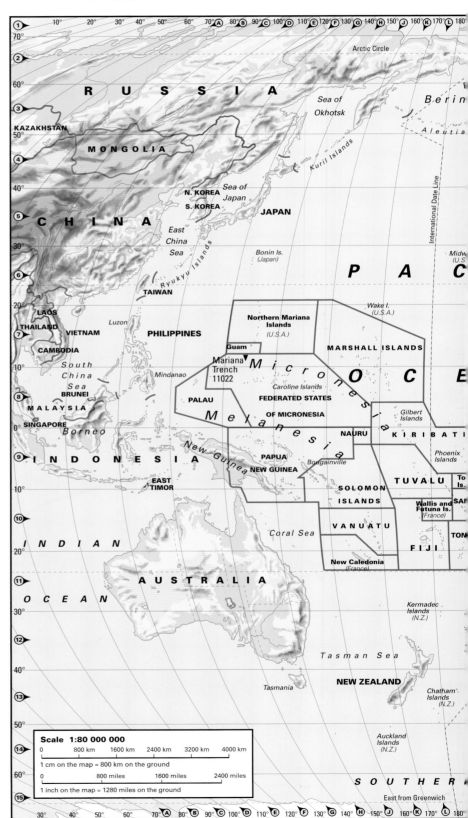

Scale 1:80 000 000

| 0 | 800 km | 1600 km | 2400 km | 3200 km | 4000 km |

1 cm on the map = 800 km on the ground

| 0 | 800 miles | 1600 miles | 2400 miles |

1 inch on the map = 1280 miles on the ground

Most islanders are occupied in farming. Many tropical crops grow well; sugar-cane, bananas and pineapples are important exports. And, with so much sea, fishing is also important. Islands big enough for a full-sized airport, such as Fiji, the Samoan islands, Tahiti, and Hawaii (see page 72), now get many tourists.

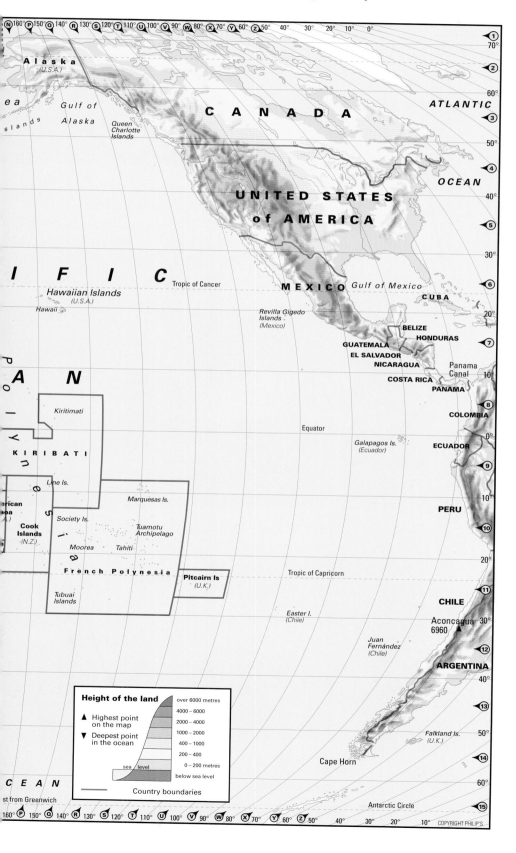

▲ **Easter Island, South Pacific.** These huge stone sculptures each weigh about 50 tonnes! They were cut long ago with simple stone axes, and lifted with ropes and ramps — an amazing achievement for people who had no metal, no wheels and no machines. Look for Easter Island on the map (in square U11): it is one of the most remote places in the world. It is now owned by Chile, 3860 kilometres away in South America.

PACIFIC FACTS

OCEAN AREA 169,500,000 sq km – the world's biggest ocean

HIGHEST POINT Mount Wilhelm (Papua New Guinea), 4508 metres

LOWEST POINT ON LAND Lake Eyre (Australia), 16 metres below sea level

DEEPEST PART OF OCEAN Mariana Trench, 11,022 metres below surface. This is the deepest place on Earth.

LONGEST RIVER Murray–Darling (Australia), 3750 km

LARGEST LAKE Lake Eyre (Australia), 8900 sq km

BIGGEST COUNTRY Australia, 7,741,220 sq km

SMALLEST COUNTRY Nauru, 21 sq km

Most Pacific countries are large groups of small islands. Their boundaries are out at sea — just lines on a map. For example, Kiribati is 33 small coral atolls spread over 5,000,000 square kilometres of ocean.

63

AUSTRALIA

AUSTRALIA

AREA 7,741,220 sq km
POPULATION 20,264,000
MONEY Australian dollar

THE GREAT BARRIER REEF

The Great Barrier Reef is the world's largest living thing! It is an area of coral over 2000 kilometres long, which grows in the warm sea near the coast of Queensland.

The reef is also home to colourful fish that swim among the coral. They can be seen from glass-bottomed boats.

AUSTRALIA is the world's largest island, but the world's smallest continent. It is the sixth-largest country in the world, smaller than the USA or Canada, but more than twice the size of India. Australia had fewer than 20 million people until recently. Most Australians are descended from people who came from Europe in the past 150 years.

Only a few people live in the mountains or in the outback – the enormous area of semi-desert and desert that makes up most of the country. The few outback people live on huge sheep and cattle farms, in mining towns, or on special reserves for the original Australians – the Aborigines. The north of Australia is tropical – and very hot.

▲ *The Flying Doctor can visit remote farms in the outback by air. The aeroplane is designed to be an ambulance, too. People in the outback use two-way radios to get medical advice, to call the doctor, and also to receive school lessons.*

▲ *Ayers Rock rises steeply out of the dry plains in central Australia. It is 348 metres high. The sides have deep gullies and strange caves. For the Aborigines, it is a holy place called Uluru. Many tourists come for the hard climb or to watch the rock glow deep red at sunset.*

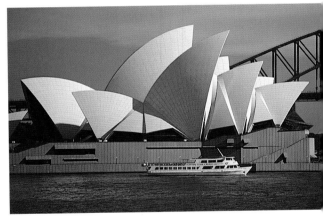

▲ *Sydney Opera House cost millions of dollars to build and has become the new symbol of Sydney. It is by the harbour, below the famous harbour bridge (in the background) which was built in Newcastle, UK!*

AUSTRALIAN ANIMALS

Australia is not joined to any other continent. It has been a separate island for millions of years, and has developed its own unique wildlife. Most of the world's marsupials live in Australia.

Australia 50c
Leadbeater's Possum
Endangered Species

Australia 30c
Bridled Nail-tailed Wallaby
Endangered Species

Australia 5c
Queensland Hairy-nosed Wombat
Endangered Species

The map shows that all the state capitals are on the coast. Canberra is a planned city built inland which became the national capital in 1927. Most Australians live near the coast and most live in towns. Sydney is by far the largest city. Even so, large areas of coast are almost uninhabited. Nullarbor ('no tree') Plain is desert by the sea.

★TRICK QUESTION: Which was the biggest island in the world, before Australia was discovered? Think very carefully – then turn to page 96.

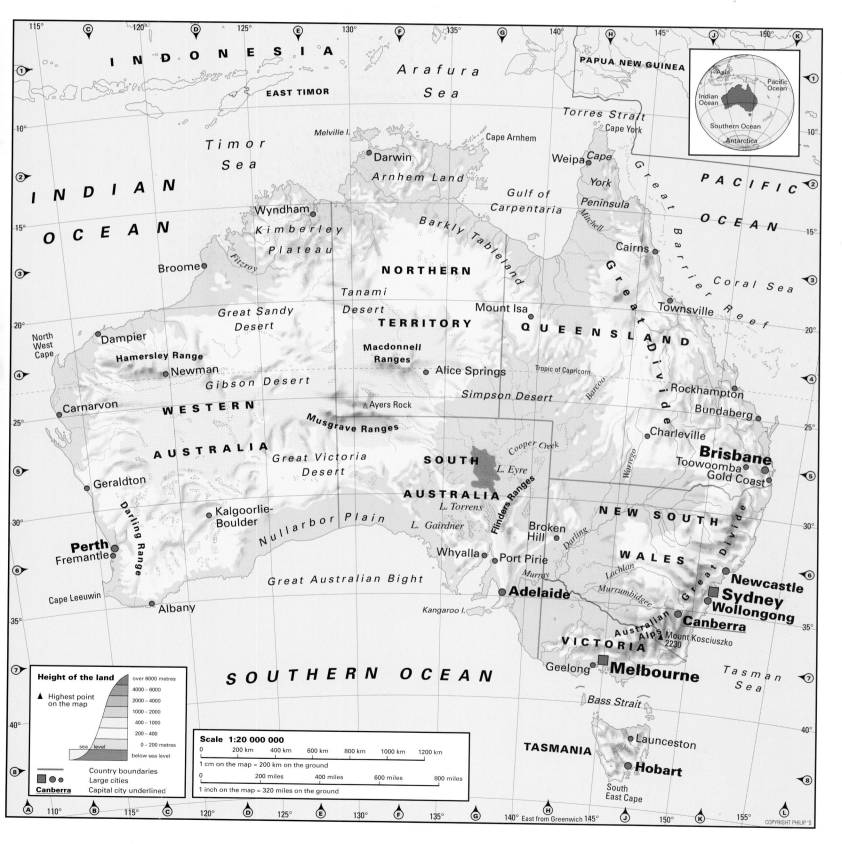

Height of the land

▲ Highest point on the map

	over 6000 metres
	4000 – 6000
	2000 – 4000
	1000 – 2000
	400 – 1000
	200 – 400
	0 – 200 metres
	below sea level

Country boundaries
Large cities
Canberra Capital city underlined

Scale 1:20 000 000

0   200 km   400 km   600 km   800 km   1000 km   1200 km

1 cm on the map = 200 km on the ground

0   200 miles   400 miles   600 miles   800 miles

1 inch on the map = 320 miles on the ground

COPYRIGHT PHILIP'S

65

NEW ZEALAND

THE ANTIPODES

New Zealand is on the opposite side of the Earth from Europe. This 'double map' is printed as if you were looking right through a transparent globe. It shows that the far north of New Zealand is at the same latitude as North Africa, and that the far south of New Zealand is at the same latitude as the centre of France. Now turn the map upside down!

THE two main islands that make up New Zealand are 2000 km east of Australia. Only 4 million people live in the whole country. The capital is Wellington, near the centre of New Zealand, but the largest city is Auckland in the north.

The original inhabitants were the Maoris, but now they are only about 8 per cent of the population. Some place-names are Maori words, such as Rotorua, Whangarei and Wanganui.

South Island is the largest island, but has fewer people than North Island. There are more sheep than people! The Canterbury Plains are a very important farming area. Aoraki Mount Cook, the highest point in New Zealand, is in the spectacular Southern Alps. Tourists visit the far south to see the glaciers and fjords. The fast-flowing rivers are used for hydro-electricity.

▲ **Auckland** is sometimes called 'the city of sails' because so many people own or sail a yacht here. The city centre (background) looks out over two huge natural harbours that are ideal for sailing. To the north is Waitemara Harbour and to the south is the shallow Manukau Harbour. Auckland is New Zealand's biggest city, and also an important port for huge container ships.

NEW ZEALAND

AREA 270,534 sq km
POPULATION 4,076,000
CURRENCY NZ dollar

KIWI FRUIT . . .

. . . **were known** as 'Chinese Gooseberries' until New Zealanders (nicknamed 'Kiwis') improved them, renamed them, and promoted them. Now they are a successful export crop for farmers, and many other countries also grow them — it is interesting to find out where YOUR kiwi fruit comes from.

▲ **The Maoris** lived in New Zealand before the Europeans came. Today, most live in North Island and many of their traditions have become part of New Zealand life. Perhaps you have seen the 'haka' on TV before an 'All Blacks' rugby game?

▲ **The Southern Alps** stretch the length of South Island. The fine scenery attracts tourists, and the grassland is used for sheep-grazing.

North Island has a warmer climate than South Island. In some places you can see hot springs and boiling mud pools and there are also volcanoes. Fine trees and giant ferns grow in the forests, but much of the forest has been cleared for farming. Cattle are kept on the rich grasslands for meat and milk. Many different kinds of fruit grow well, including apples, kiwi fruit and pears, which are exported.

On the map below you can find: a sea and a bay named after the Dutch explorer, Abel Tasman; a strait (sea channel) and a mountain named after the British explorer, James Cook.

GEOTHERMAL POWER

Geothermal power station, north of Lake Taupo, North Island. In this volcanic area, there is very hot water underground. When drilled, it gushes out as steam. This can be piped to a power station (above) to generate electricity. Hot steam gushing out of a natural hole is called a geyser (below).

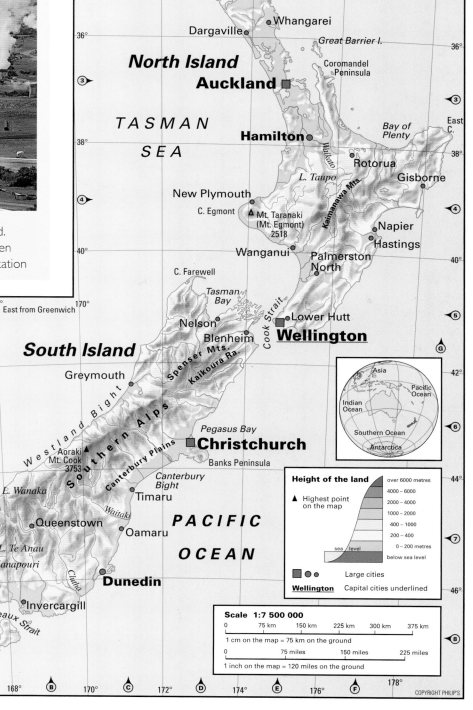

67

NORTH AMERICA

NORTH America includes many Arctic islands, a huge mainland area (quite narrow in Central America) and the islands in the Caribbean Sea. The map shows the great mountain ranges, including the Rockies, which are the most impressive feature of this continent.

Almost all of the west is high and mountainous, yet Death Valley is *below* sea level. The rocks have been folded into mountain ranges, but the highest peaks are volcanoes. The Appalachian Mountains in the east are also fold mountains. And the island chains of the north-west (the Aleutian Islands) and the south-east (the West Indies) are the tops of underwater ranges divided by shallow seas.

The political map of North America is quite a simple one. The boundary between Canada and the USA is mostly at exactly 49°N. Four of the five Great Lakes have one shore in Canada and one shore in the USA★. Canada's two biggest cities, Toronto and Montreal, are south of the 49° line! Find them on the map on page 71.

Greenland used to be a colony of Denmark, but now it is self-governing. Most of Greenland is covered by ice all year. See page 88 for more about Greenland and the Arctic Ocean, and page 73 for Alaska (which is part of the USA).

★ *Which lakes? Answers on page 96.*

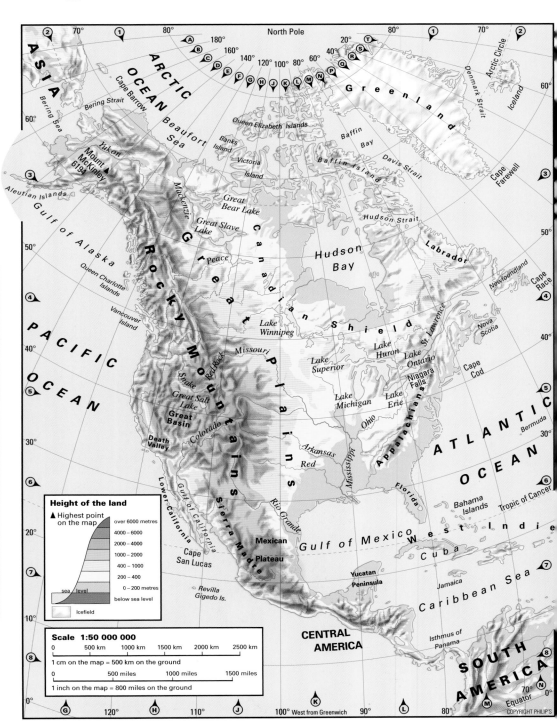

▲ *Flyovers, Los Angeles, USA. There are three levels of road at this road junction in Los Angeles; sometimes there are traffic jams as well! In 1994, a huge earthquake destroyed many road bridges.*

Height of the land

▲ Highest point on the map

over 6000 metres
4000 – 6000
2000 – 4000
1000 – 2000
400 – 1000
200 – 400
0 – 200 metres
sea / level
below sea level

icefield

Scale 1:50 000 000

0   500 km   1000 km   1500 km   2000 km   2500 km

1 cm on the map = 500 km on the ground

0   500 miles   1000 miles   1500 miles

1 inch on the map = 800 miles on the ground

Mexico and the seven countries of **Central America** have more complicated boundaries. Six of these countries have two coastlines. The map shows that one country has a coastline only on the Pacific Ocean, and one has a coastline only on the Caribbean Sea★. These countries are Spanish-speaking: in fact there are more Spanish speakers here than in Spain.

The **West Indies** are made up of islands; there are lots of countries too. Cuba is the biggest island country. One island has TWO countries on it★. They are shown in more detail on page 81. This area is often called 'The Caribbean'. Some West Indians have emigrated to the USA, Britain and France.

★ *Which ones? Answers on page 96.*

▲ *Market in St George's, Grenada.*
The West Indies have hot sunshine and plenty of rain. This is an ideal climate for growing vegetables and fruit. These stalls are stacked high with local produce. Many islands have volcanic soil which is rich in minerals and very fertile.

Grenada is an island country which grows and exports bananas and nutmeg. Find it on the map on page 81.

NORTH AMERICA FACTS

AREA 24,249,000 sq km
HIGHEST POINT Mount McKinley (Alaska), 6194 metres
LOWEST POINT Death Valley (California), 86 metres below sea level
LONGEST RIVERS
 Red Rock–Missouri–Mississippi, 5970 km
 Mackenzie–Peace, 4240 km
LARGEST LAKE Lake Superior*, 82,350 sq km
BIGGEST COUNTRY
 Canada, 9,970,610 sq km
SMALLEST COUNTRY Grenada (West Indies), 344 sq km
RICHEST COUNTRY USA
POOREST COUNTRY Haiti
MOST CROWDED COUNTRY Barbados
LEAST CROWDED COUNTRY Canada

* The world's largest freshwater lake

69

CANADA

CANADA

AREA 9,970,610 sq km
POPULATION 33,099,000
MONEY Canadian dollar
CAPITAL Ottawa

STAMPS

This stamp is an air-picture of the prairies of central Canada. The huge flat fields of grain reach to the far horizon, and beyond.

In western Canada, the Rocky Mountains are high and jagged. There are glaciers among the peaks. The Rockies stretch for 4800 km through both Canada and the USA. They were a great barrier to the early explorers and to the early settlers, railway engineers and road builders.

ONLY one country in the world is bigger than Canada★, but 30 countries have more people than Canada. Most of Canada is almost empty. Some of the northern islands are uninhabited. Very few people live in the Northwest Territories, or in the western mountains, or near Hudson Bay. The farmland of the prairies (see the top stamp) is uncrowded too. So . . . where do Canadians live?

The answer is that more Canadians live in cities than in the countryside. The map shows where the biggest cities are – all of them are in the southern part of Canada, and none are as far north as Norway or Sweden in Europe. Toronto is on the same latitude as Venice and Milan.

These photographs show Canada in summer. In winter, it is very cold indeed in both central and northern Canada. Children go to school even when it is 40° below zero. The mildest winters are in the south-west, around Vancouver.

★ *Which country? See page 9.*

▲ *Quebec City. The Chateau Frontenac (seen on the left) is built in the style of a French chateau (castle). This part of Canada was once owned by the French, and the people still speak French. On the right is the port beside the River St Lawrence. Large ocean-going ships can dock here.*

▲ *The Niagara Falls are between Lake Erie and Lake Ontario, on the border of the USA (in the distance) and Canada. One part is called the Horseshoe Falls: can you see why? Ships have to use a canal with locks to get past the falls. The falling water is used to generate hydro-electricity.*

▲ *A long-distance train travels through a pass in the Rocky Mountains. The trans-Canada railway helped to unite Canada as one country.*

LANGUAGES IN CANADA

Canada has two official languages: French and English. So Canadian stamps say 'Postes/Postage', instead of only 'Postage'. Most of the French-speaking Canadians live in the province of Quebec, which once belonged to France.

The biggest city in Quebec is Montreal: it is four times as big as Ottawa, the capital of Canada.

▲ **Vancouver, British Columbia:** *the biggest city in the west of Canada.*

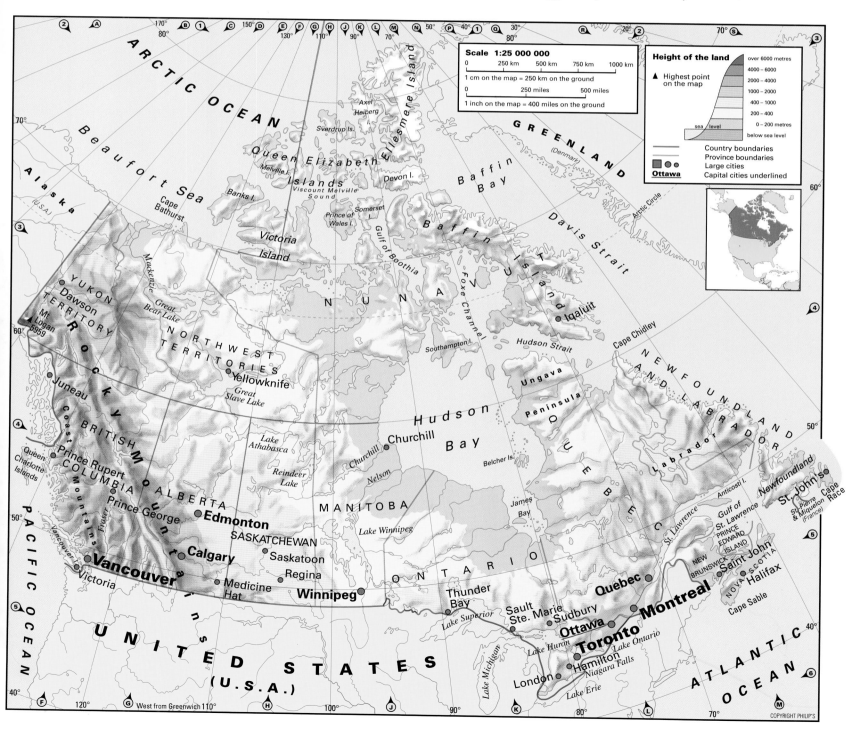

Scale 1:25 000 000

1 cm on the map = 250 km on the ground

1 inch on the map = 400 miles on the ground

Height of the land
- over 6000 metres
- 4000 – 6000
- 2000 – 4000
- 1000 – 2000
- 400 – 1000
- 200 – 400
- 0 – 200 metres
- below sea level

▲ Highest point on the map

sea level

Country boundaries
Province boundaries
Large cities
Ottawa Capital cities underlined

71

USA

WHO are 'the Americans'? Of every 100 people in the USA, over 80 have ancestors from Europe. The first colonists came from Britain, France and Spain, but later on, people came from almost all parts of Europe to the USA.

About 12 people out of every 100 came from West Africa, brought to the USA as slaves to work in the southern states. By 1865, the slaves were free. Many black Americans now live in the north-east. More recently, many Spanish-speaking people have arrived from Mexico and Puerto Rico.

There are now fewer than one million American Indians in the USA, some of whom live on special reservations.

▲ **American football:** the Baltimore Ravens and the New York Giants have both travelled over 1400 kilometres to Tampa, Florida, for this big game. Their supporters fill the huge stadium.

STARS AND STRIPES

United States 13c

In 1776 there were only 13 states in the USA: so the US flag had 13 stars and 13 stripes. As more and more states joined

the USA, more stars were added to the flag. Now there are 50 states, and 50 stars.

HAWAII

Hawaii
is the newest state in the USA: it became a state in 1959. The picture shows Waikiki beach in Honolulu, the biggest city. Honolulu is on Oahu island. These faraway Pacific islands are the tops of volcanoes, over 3000 km from mainland USA (see map page 63). Hawaii island itself has a very active volcano in the south. If the height of Mauna Kea is measured from the seabed, it is 10,023 metres: the world's highest mountain. The islands are the most southerly part of the USA.

STAMP

First Moon Landing, 1969

An American was the first man on the Moon in 1969. The astronaut is holding the USA flag. Above his head is the Earth, half in darkness.

USA

AREA 9,629,091 sq km
POPULATION 298,444,000
MONEY US dollar
CAPITAL Washington, DC

The map shows the 50 states of the USA. The first 13 states were on the east coast, settled by Europeans who had sailed across the Atlantic. As the Americans moved westwards, so more states were formed. The western states are bigger than the states in the east. You can see their straight boundaries on the map: those boundaries were drawn *before* the settlers arrived.

DISTANCE CHART

Read the chart just like a tables-chart, or a graph. The distance chart shows how big the USA is. How far is it from Seattle to Miami? Or from New Orleans to Chicago? (Answers on page 96.)

Road distances in km	New York	Miami	Chicago	New Orleans	Seattle
Miami	2138				
Chicago	1346	2198			
New Orleans	2131	1406	1488		
Seattle	4613	5445	3288	4211	
San Francisco	4850	4915	3499	3622	1352

ALASKA

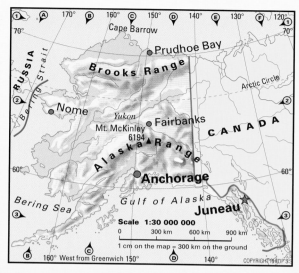

Alaska is the biggest state of the USA – but it has the fewest people. It was bought from Russia in 1867 for $7 million: the best bargain ever, particularly as oil was discovered a hundred years later. Oil has helped Alaska to become rich. Timber and fish are the other main products. Much of Alaska is mountainous or covered in forest. In the north, there is darkness all day in December, and months of ice-cold weather. But in the short summer, visitors love the long days and short nights. Farming is not possible in most of Alaska – except in the far south.

DID YOU KNOW? The Bering Strait is the only sea route from the Pacific to the Arctic Ocean, but it is often frozen over.

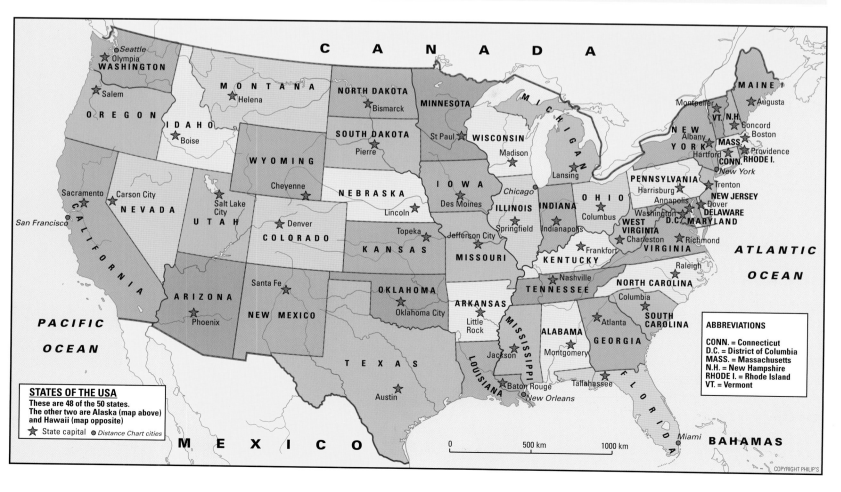

STATES OF THE USA
These are 48 of the 50 states.
The other two are Alaska (map above) and Hawaii (map opposite)
★ State capital   ● Distance Chart cities

ABBREVIATIONS
CONN. = Connecticut
D.C. = District of Columbia
MASS. = Massachusetts
N.H. = New Hampshire
RHODE I. = Rhode Island
VT. = Vermont

EASTERN USA

▲ **The Statue of Liberty** stands on an island in New York harbour. When people arrived by ship, the statue was there to greet them! The torch at the top is 93 metres above the ground.

THE map shows only half the USA, but over three-quarters of the population live in this half of the country.

The great cities of the north-east were the first big industrial areas in America. Pittsburgh's American football team is still called the Pittsburgh Steelers, even though many of the steelworks have closed down.

In recent years, many people have moved from the 'snow-belt' of the north to the 'sun-belt' of the south. New industries are booming in the south, where once there was much poverty. And many older people retire to Florida, where even midwinter feels almost like summer. But beware of hurricanes in the summer!

In the south of the USA it is hot enough for cotton, tobacco and peanuts to be successful crops. The palm tree on the flag of South Carolina (below, right) suggests that the climate of this part of America is nearly tropical. Summers are very hot and humid and winters are mostly mild.

The Appalachian Mountains are beautiful, especially in the fall (autumn), when the leaves of the trees turn red. But this area is the poorest part of the USA. Coal mines have closed and farmland is poor. The good farmland is west of the Appalachians, where you can drive for hundreds of kilometres past wheat and sweetcorn.

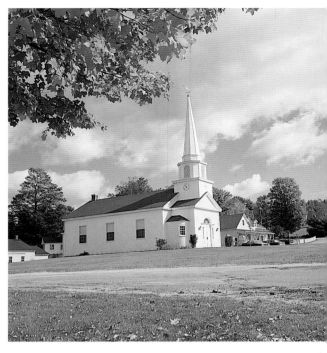

▲ **Canterbury Church, New Hampshire.** *The north-east corner of the USA is called New England and was settled by English colonists. This church by the village green is very like old England! The settlers named their towns and villages after places they had known in England.*

WHICH US CITY IS MOST IMPORTANT?

Washington, DC, is the capital city, where the President lives. But New York has far more people and industries than Washington. So *both* are the most important city – but in different ways.

▲ **Skyscrapers in Chicago,** *the biggest inland city in the USA. The world's first skyscraper was built here in 1885. These skyscrapers look out over Lake Michigan. The lake shore can freeze over in winter.*

Every US state has its own flag: six state flags are on the page opposite. Several states were named after kings and queens of England – in the days when these states were English colonies. For example, CAROLina (North and South) use the Latin name for King Charles I; MARYland is named after his wife, Queen Mary, and GEORGia is named after King George II. But LOUISiana is named after King Louis XIV of France because France colonized a vast area along the Mississippi river.

GREAT LAKES

Try using the first letters of the Great Lakes to make a sentence:

Superior	**S**uper
Michigan	**M**an
Huron	**H**elps
Erie	**E**very
Ontario	**O**ne

Now you'll *never* forget the west-to-east order of the Great Lakes!

THE MISSISSIPPI

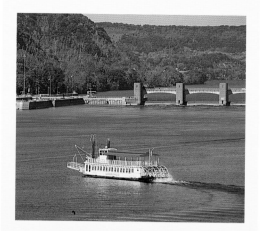

The Mississippi River was known as the 'Great River Road' because it was an important route into the heart of the USA. 'Stern-wheeler' paddle-steamers

travelled the river with cargoes. It is still an important river today. Dams (above) and locks make it easier for big barges to use the river. The dams also help to reduce the risk of floods.

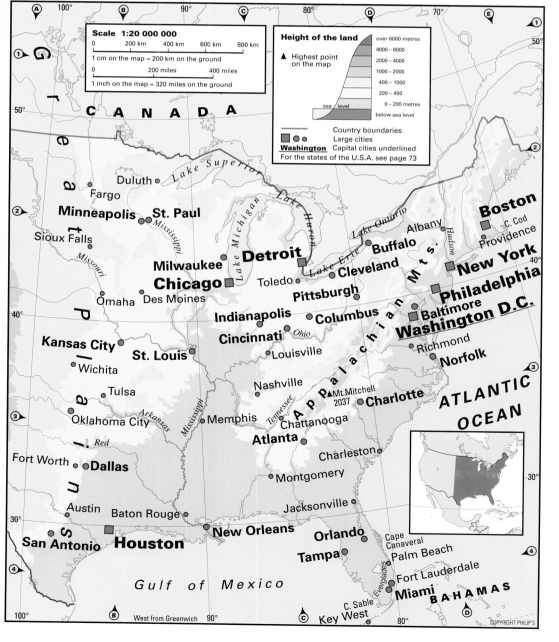

▲ *Performing whales at Orlando, Florida.* These killer whales have been trained to perform to the audience. Florida is a popular state for holidays. Orlando is one of the world's most popular tourist resorts, with Disney World and other theme parks.

WESTERN USA

CALIFORNIA

COLORADO

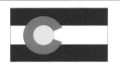

SOUTH DAKOTA

MANY parts of the western USA have hardly any people. The Rocky Mountains are beautiful for holidays, but it is hard to make a living there.

The only big city on the high plateaus west of the Rockies is Salt Lake City, Utah, which was settled by the Mormons. Some former mining towns are now 'ghost towns': when the mines closed, all the people left. The toughest area of all is the desert land of Arizona in the south-west. The mountains and deserts were a great problem to the pioneers, but today the spectacular scenery and wildlife are preserved in large national parks.

▲ *The 'Wild West'.* Scenes like this one are rare now, except when they are put on for the many tourists who visit the area. But in the days of the 'Wild West', 100 years or more ago, the skills of cowboys were vital. Look carefully – this picture shows a cowgirl *rounding up horses!*

▲ *Wheat harvest, USA.* A huge combine harvester moves across a field of wheat. Up to 150 years ago, this land was covered in grass and grazed by buffaloes. Much of this wheat will go abroad.

WHAT DO THE NAMES MEAN?

The Spanish were the first settlers in the western USA, and they have left us many Spanish names. Can you match the name and its meaning? (*Answers on page 96.*)

Amarillo (*Texas*)	The pass
Colorado	Yellow
El Paso (*Texas*)	The angels
Los Angeles	St Francis
San Jose	Coloured
San Francisco	St Joseph

Energy conservation. A great idea! But Americans use more energy than anyone else in the world.

WYOMING

ARIZONA

WASHINGTON

NEBRASKA

OKLAHOMA

TEXAS

▲ *Grand Canyon, Arizona.* The Colorado River has cut a huge canyon 1½ kilometres deep and several kilometres wide in this desert area of the USA. The mountains slowly rose, while the river kept carving a deeper valley.

The Great Plains east of the Rocky Mountains are flat but high. Denver has the 'Mile-high Stadium'! These dry plains have enormous cattle ranches. Where there is enough rain, crops of wheat and sweetcorn (maize) stretch to the horizon.

The Pacific coastlands of the north-west have plenty of rain and the climate is quite like north-west Europe. The mountains and valleys are thickly forested and timber is an important product. Seattle is on a sheltered inlet of the sea.

CALIFORNIA

California now has more people than any other state, and it is the USA's 'hi-tech' centre. It has many advantages. In the Central Valley, the climate is right for many crops: oranges from California are well known, and grapes grow well and are made into wine. The desert of the south is attractive to retired people – many people migrate here from all over the USA.

▲ **A street-car in San Francisco.** Street-cars still climb the steep hills in San Francisco, California. A moving cable runs beneath the street. The car is fixed to the cable and starts with a jerk! In the background you can see an inlet of the Pacific and Alcatraz – once a top-security prison island.

▲ **Hollywood** is a suburb of Los Angeles. Rich film-stars live here in expensive houses. The clear blue skies and lack of rain were helpful to film-makers. But now, Los Angeles has so many cars there is more smog from pollution than clear skies.

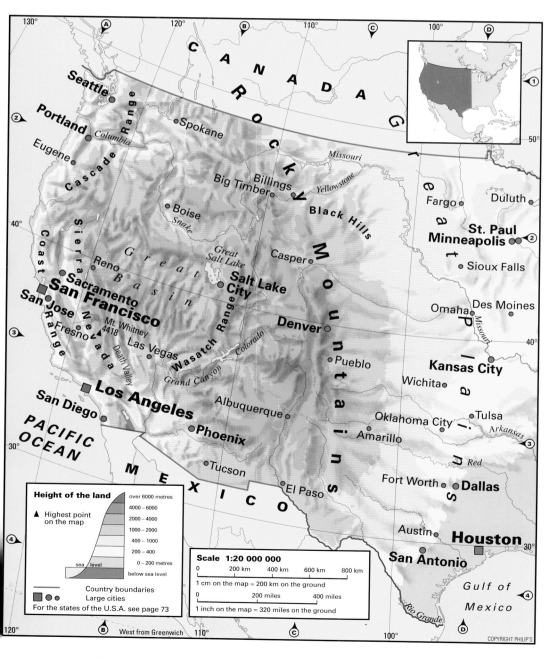

Height of the land
- over 6000 metres
- 4000 – 6000
- 2000 – 4000
- 1000 – 2000
- 400 – 1000
- 200 – 400
- 0 – 200 metres
- below sea level
- ▲ Highest point on the map
- sea level

Country boundaries
Large cities
For the states of the U.S.A. see page 73

Scale 1:20 000 000
0 — 200 km — 400 km — 600 km — 800 km
1 cm on the map = 200 km on the ground
0 — 200 miles — 400 miles
1 inch on the map = 320 miles on the ground

COPYRIGHT PHILIP'S

CENTRAL AMERICA

MEXICO

AREA 1,958,201 sq km
POPULATION 107,450,000
MONEY New peso

GUATEMALA

AREA 108,889 sq km
POPULATION 12,294,000
MONEY Quetzal

PANAMA

AREA 75,517 sq km
POPULATION 3,191,000
MONEY Balboa

MEXICO is by far the most important country on this map. Over 107 million people live in Mexico – more than in any country in Europe. Mexico City has a population of about 15 million: it is one of the biggest cities in the world. A major earthquake did much damage there in 1985.

Most Mexicans live on the high plateau of central Mexico. Industries are growing fast in Mexico City and near the border with the USA. There are very few people in the northern desert, in Lower California in the north-west, in the southern jungle, or in Yucatan in the east. But tourist resorts thrive on the Yucatan and Pacific coasts.

The other seven countries on this map are quite small. None of them has as many people as Mexico City! These countries were once ruled by Spain, but they have been independent since the 1820s. Civil wars have caused many problems in Central America. But the climate is good for growing many tropical crops, so lots of forest has been cut down for farmland.

▲ **Ruins at Chichen Itza, Mexico.** *Great temples were built by the people known as Mayas over a thousand years ago. These amazing ruins are in Yucatan, the most easterly part of Mexico. The tourists look tiny, which shows you how HUGE the pyramid is. Today, this is an area of jungle.*

BELIZE

AREA 22,966 sq km
POPULATION 288,000
MONEY Belize dollar

TORTILLAS – A RECIPE FOR YOU TO COOK

Ingredients
225 grams of maize flour (sweetcorn flour)
salt and water

Method
1 Mix the maize flour, salt and water into a soft dough.
2 Pat into round shapes about ½ centimetre thick, and 12 centimetres across.
3 Melt a little margarine in a frying-pan.
4 Place the tortillas in the hot frying-pan.
5 For best results, turn the tortillas over.
6 Serve at once!
You have now cooked one of the most important meals of Central America. Maize (sweetcorn) was developed as a crop in the Americas, and is now grown in many parts of the world. You eat maize often as Corn Flakes and semolina.

▲ **The Toucan** *is sometimes called the 'banana-beak bird', for an obvious reason! It eats fruit and lives in the forest, nesting in a hole in a tree. If the forest is cleared, it will have nowhere to live.*

THE PANAMA CANAL

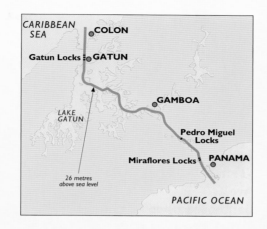

PANAMA CANAL CROSS-SECTION

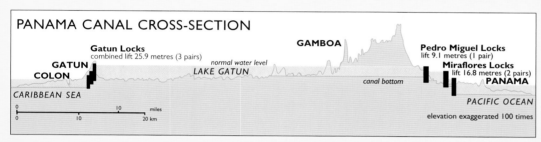

The Panama Canal links the Caribbean Sea with the Pacific Ocean. It was opened in 1914. Many workers died of fever while digging the canal through the jungle. It is 82 km long, and the deepest cutting is 82 metres deep – the world's biggest 'ditch'!

There are six locks along the route of the canal. The photograph (left) shows two ships travelling through the canal. The map and diagram show that part of the route is through Lake Gatun, at 26 metres above sea level. So the ships have to pass through three locks at each end.

Over 15,000 ships use the canal each year, and sometimes there are 'traffic jams' at the locks: it is the busiest big-ship canal in the world. Before the Panama Canal was built, the only sea route from the Pacific to the Atlantic was round South America.

In which direction are ships travelling from the Caribbean to the Pacific? Does this surprise you? Look at the map below.

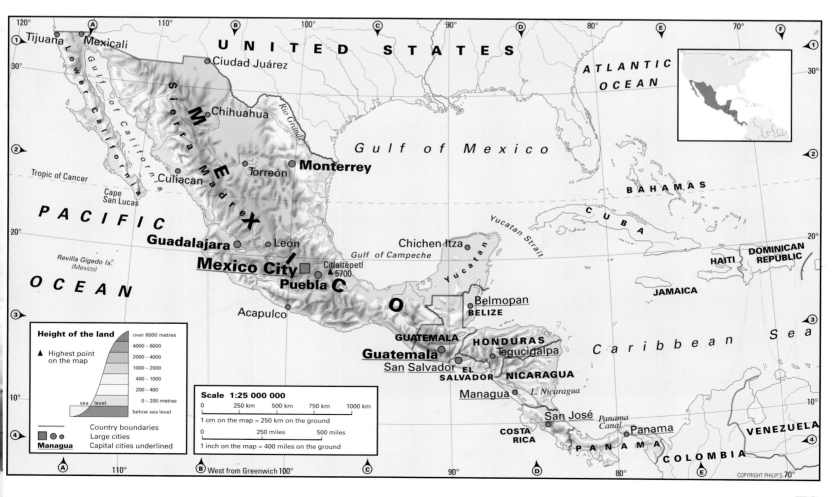

SOUTH AMERICA

A TOUR of South America would be very exciting. At the Equator are the hot steamy jungles of the Amazon lowlands. To the west comes the great climb up to the Andes Mountains – the world's longest mountain chain. The peaks are so high that even the volcanoes are snow-capped all year. Travellers on buses and trains are offered extra oxygen to breathe, because the air is so thin.

Squeezed between the Andes and the Pacific Ocean in Peru and northern Chile is the world's driest desert – the Atacama Desert, which stretches southwards from the border with Peru for nearly 1600 kilometres. Very few people live here.

Further south in Chile are more wet forests – but these forests are cool. The monkey-puzzle tree originates here. But eastwards, in Argentina, there is less rain and more grass. Cattle on the Pampas are rounded up by cowboys, and crops such as corn (maize) grow well. Further south is the very cold and dry area called Patagonia where sheep farming is important.

▲ **Reed boats on Lake Titicaca,** the highest navigable lake in the world. It is high in the Andes, at 3811 metres above sea level. Totora reeds grow around the shores, and the Indians tie bundles of reeds together to make fishing boats. The picture shows the reed shelters they use while they make the boats and go fishing. In the background you can see a mountain rising from the plateau.

Lake Titicaca is shared between Peru and Bolivia. A steam-powered ferry boat travels the length of the lake.

Why is Lake Titicaca the only stretch of water available for the Bolivian navy? (Check the map!)

Height of the land

▲ Highest point on the map

over 6000 metres
4000 – 6000
2000 – 4000
1000 – 2000
400 – 1000
200 – 400
0 – 200 metres
below sea level

sea level

Scale 1:40 000 000

0   400 km   800 km   1200 km   1600 km   2000 km

1 cm on the map = 400 km on the ground

0   400 miles   800 miles   1200 miles

1 inch on the map = 640 miles on the ground

COPYRIGHT PHILIP'S

South America stretches further south than any other continent (apart from Antarctica). The cold and stormy tip of South America, Cape Horn, is only 1000 kilometres from Antarctica.

In every South American country, the population is growing fast. Most of the farmland is owned by a few rich people, and many people are desperately poor. Young people are leaving the countryside for the cities, most of which are encircled by shanty towns. There is rapid progress in the big cities, but many people do not benefit.

ONE country occupies nearly half the total area of South America, and has over half the population of the whole continent: BRAZIL. Look at the map to see which countries touch Brazil. Which two do not?

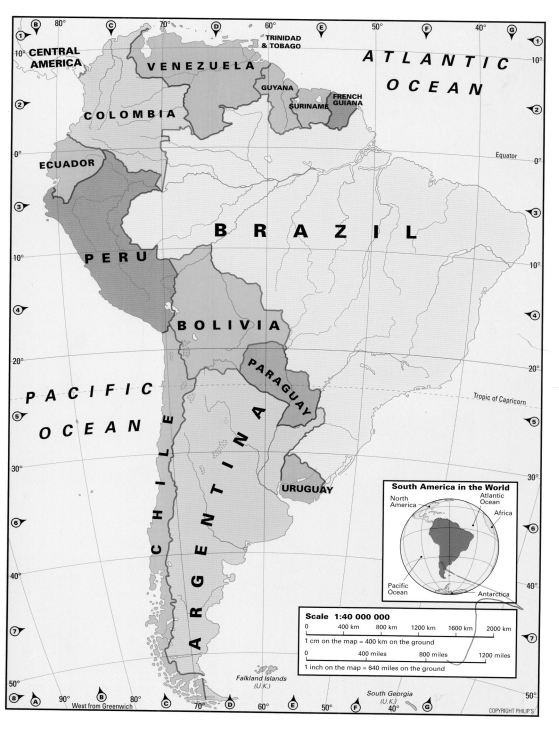

▲ **Carnival in Rio de Janeiro, Brazil.**
Rio de Janeiro is the second-largest city of Brazil. Every year, it bursts into life and colour at carnival time, in February or March. Huge processions of decorated floats and dancers parade through the streets. Poor people from the shanty towns enjoy it as much as the rich people who pay for seats on the special stands.

SOUTH AMERICA FACTS

AREA 17,600,000 sq km
HIGHEST POINT Mount Aconcagua (Argentina), 6960 metres
LOWEST POINT Valdés Peninsula (Argentina), −40 metres
LONGEST RIVER Amazon, 6450 km
LARGEST LAKE Lake Titicaca (Bolivia and Peru), 8285 sq km
BIGGEST COUNTRY Brazil, 8,514,215 sq km
SMALLEST COUNTRY Suriname*, 163,265 sq km
RICHEST COUNTRY Venezuela
POOREST COUNTRY Guyana
MOST CROWDED COUNTRY Ecuador
LEAST CROWDED COUNTRY Suriname
HIGHEST WATERFALL Angel Falls, 979 metres (a world record)
* French Guiana is smaller, but it is not independent

83

TROPICAL SOUTH AMERICA

COLOMBIA

AREA 1,138,914 sq km
POPULATION 43,593,000
MONEY Peso

ECUADOR

AREA 283,561 sq km
POPULATION 13,548,000
MONEY US dollar

BRAZIL

AREA 8,514,215 sq km
POPULATION 188,078,000
MONEY Real

BRAZIL is by far the biggest country in South America, and has more people (over 188 million) than the rest of South America put together.

Most people still live near the coast. Parts of the Amazon forest are now being settled, but large areas inland are still almost empty. The poorest parts are in the north-east, where the rains often fail, and in the shanty towns around the cities. Modern industry is growing very fast, but there are still too few jobs. Brazil has pioneered fuel made from sugar-cane for cars and trucks.

Colombia, Ecuador, Peru and Bolivia are known as the Andean states. **Colombia** is known for its coffee. Bananas and other tropical crops grow near the coast of **Ecuador**, but the capital city is high in the mountains. **Peru** relies on mountain rivers to bring water to the dry coastal area. Tourists come to see ancient Inca cities. **Bolivia** has the highest capital city in the world. It is the poorest country in South America: farming is difficult and even the tin mines hardly make a profit.

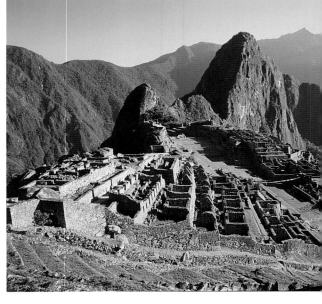

▲ **Machu Picchu, Peru,** the lost city of the Incas, is perched on a mountainside 2400 metres above sea level. The last Inca emperor probably lived here in 1580. The ruins were rediscovered in 1911.

PERU

AREA 1,285,216 sq km
POPULATION 28,303,000
MONEY New sol

▲ **Going to market, Peru.** This lady is a descendant of the Incas who lived in Peru before the Spanish arrived. She carries her baby on her back in a fine woven blanket. In most South American countries, the Indians are among the poorest people.

▲ **Amazon jungle.** The hot, wet jungle covers thousands of kilometres. There is no cool season, and the forest is always green. The trees can be 50 metres high. New roads and villages, mines and dams are being built in the Brazilian jungle, and parts of the forest are being destroyed.

THE GALAPAGOS ISLANDS

These volcanic islands belong to Ecuador but are 1000 kilometres from the mainland. They have unique plants and animals because they have been isolated for so long. The giant tortoises are the most famous and spectacular 'residents'.

Venezuela is the richest country in South America because of its mineral wealth. Oil is pumped up from beneath Lake Maracaibo, and iron ore is mined from the plateau south of the River Orinoco. The world's highest waterfall, the Angel Falls, is in Venezuela.

In Guyana there are important deposits of bauxite, which is used to make aluminium. Guyana was once British Guiana, and Suriname was once Dutch Guiana. But French Guiana is *still* French.

DID YOU KNOW?

Ecuador means *Equator*: the Equator (0°) crosses the country

Colombia is named after Christopher Columbus, who sailed from Europe to the Americas in 1492

Bolivia is named after Simon Bolivar, a hero of the country's war of independence in the 1820s

La Paz, in Bolivia, means *peace*

▲ *Cattle and cowboys* in the Mato Grosso, in Brazil. This huge area of dry woodland and grassland is used to graze cattle. Horses are used to round them up.

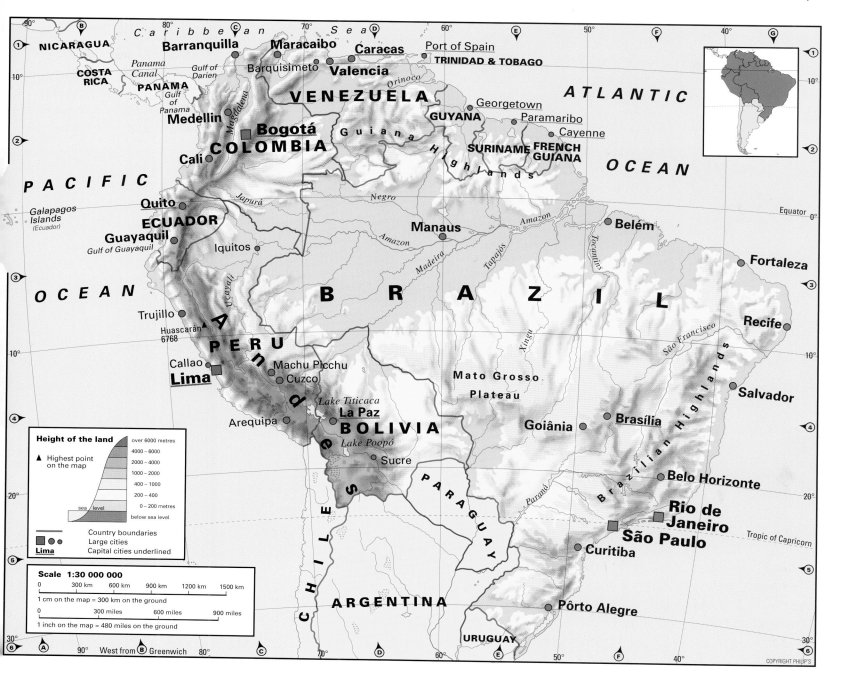

Height of the land

▲ Highest point on the map

- over 6000 metres
- 4000 – 6000
- 2000 – 4000
- 1000 – 2000
- 400 – 1000
- 200 – 400
- 0 – 200 metres
- below sea level

sea level

Country boundaries
Large cities
Lima Capital cities underlined

Scale 1:30 000 000

0   300 km   600 km   900 km   1200 km   1500 km

1 cm on the map = 300 km on the ground

0   300 miles   600 miles   900 miles

1 inch on the map = 480 miles on the ground

NICARAGUA
COSTA RICA
PANAMA
Panama Canal
Gulf of Darien
Barranquilla
Maracaibo
Caracas
Port of Spain
TRINIDAD & TOBAGO
Barquisimeto
Valencia
Orinoco
VENEZUELA
Gulf of Panama
Medellin
Bogotá
COLOMBIA
Guiana
Cali
Georgetown
GUYANA
Paramaribo
Cayenne
SURINAME
FRENCH GUIANA
Highlands
ATLANTIC
OCEAN
PACIFIC
Quito
ECUADOR
Galapagos Islands (Ecuador)
Guayaquil
Gulf of Guayaquil
Japurá
Negro
Amazon
Manaus
Amazon
Belém
Equator
Iquitos
OCEAN
Madeira
Tapajós
Tocantins
Fortaleza
B R A Z I L
Trujillo
Huascarán 6768
PERU
Recife
São Francisco
Callao
Machu Picchu
Cuzco
Lima
Xingu
Mato Grosso Plateau
Salvador
Lake Titicaca
La Paz
BOLIVIA
Lake Poopó
Arequipa
Sucre
Goiânia
Brasília
Brazilian Highlands
Belo Horizonte
Paraná
PARAGUAY
CHILE
Rio de Janeiro
São Paulo
Tropic of Capricorn
Curitiba
ARGENTINA
Pôrto Alegre
URUGUAY

West from Greenwich

COPYRIGHT PHILIP'S

85

TEMPERATE SOUTH AMERICA

ARGENTINA

AREA 2,780,400 sq km
POPULATION 39,922,000
MONEY Argentine peso

CHILE

AREA 756,626 sq km
POPULATION 16,134,000
MONEY Chilean peso

URUGUAY

AREA 175,016 sq km
POPULATION 3,432,000
MONEY Uruguayan peso

CHILE is 4300 kilometres long, but it is only about 200 kilometres wide, because it is sandwiched between the Andes and the Pacific.

In the north is the Atacama Desert, the driest in the world. In one place, there was no rain for 400 years! Fortunately, rivers from the Andes permit some irrigation. Chilean nitrates come from this area. Nitrates are salts in dried-up lakes; they are used to make fertilizers and explosives. Copper is mined high in the mountains.

In the centre, the climate is like the Mediterranean area and California, with hot dry summers and warm wet winters with westerly winds. This is a lovely climate, and most Chileans live in this area.

In the south, Chile is wet, windy and cool. Thick forests which include the Chilean pine (monkey-puzzle tree) cover the steep hills. The reason for these contrasts is the wind. It rains when westerly winds blow from the Pacific Ocean. These westerly winds blow all year in the south, but only in winter in the centre, and not at all in the north.

▲ **Geysers in the Andes, Chile.** *Hot steam hisses into the cold air, 4000 metres above sea level in the Andes of northern Chile. It shows there is still plenty of volcanic activity in the Andes.*

PARAGUAY

AREA 406,752 sq km
POPULATION 6,506,000
MONEY Guarani

STAMP

The monkey-puzzle tree comes from Chile. Its proper name is the Chilean pine. The branches are a spiral of very sharp pointed leaves. The cones have tasty seeds. It was called 'monkey-puzzle' tree because to climb it would even puzzle a monkey!

THE ANDES

The Andes are over 7000 kilometres long, so they are the longest mountain range in the world. They are fold mountains, with a very steep western side, and a gentler eastern side. Most of the high peaks are volcanoes: they are the highest volcanoes in the world. Mount Aconcagua (6960 metres) is extinct. Mount Guallatiri, in Chile, is the world's highest active volcano.

The higher you climb, the cooler it is. And the further you travel from the Equator, the cooler it is. Therefore, the snowline in southern Chile is much lower than in northern Chile, and in the far south glaciers reach the sea.

▲ **Sheep farming in Patagonia, Argentina.** *Southern Argentina has a cool, dry climate. Very few people live there – but lots of sheep roam the extensive grasslands. There are almost as many sheep in Argentina as there are people.*

Argentina is the world's eighth largest country. Its name means 'silvery' in Spanish: some of the early settlers came to mine silver. But today, Argentina's most important product is cattle. Cool grasslands called the Pampas (see map below) are ideal for cattle-grazing.

Argentina is a varied country: the north-west is hot and dry, and the south is cold and dry. The frontier with Chile runs high along the top of the Andes.

Buenos Aires, the capital city, is the biggest city in South America; it has 11 million people. The name means 'good air', but petrol fumes have now polluted the air.

Paraguay and **Uruguay** are two countries with small populations: you can find the details near the flags on page 86. Nearly half the population of Uruguay lives in the capital city, Montevideo, which is on the coast. In contrast Paraguay is a landlocked country. Find its capital on the map. Animal farming is the most important occupation in both these countries.

All these four countries – Chile, Argentina, Paraguay and Uruguay – have Spanish as their official language. Most of the people have European ancestors, except in Paraguay where there are a lot of South American Indians.

THE FALKLAND ISLANDS

Port Stanley, capital of the Falklands, looks similar to an English town. These islands are a British colony in the South Atlantic with about 3000 people living there. They are about 480 km east of Argentina, which claims them as the Islas Malvinas. Britain fought an Argentine invasion in 1982. Sheep farming and fishing are the main occupations, and the islands want more tourists to visit.

▲ **Santiago, capital of Chile,** has a beautiful setting between the Andes and the coastal mountains. A third of Chile's people live in Santiago. Its name means 'St James' – the patron saint of Spain, which once ruled Chile.

87

THE ARCTIC

THE Arctic is an ocean surrounding the North Pole. It is frozen all through the winter and still has lots of ice in summer. It is surrounded by the northernmost areas of three continents, but Greenland is the only truly Arctic country.

For most of the year the land is snow-covered. During the short summer, when the sun never sets, the snow and the frozen topsoil melt. But the deeper soil is still frozen, so the land is very marshy. This treeless landscape is called the tundra. Reindeer and caribou can be herded or hunted, but farming is impossible.

In recent years, oil and other rich mineral deposits have been found. Canada, the USA and Russia have military bases near the Arctic Ocean.

From the Atlantic Ocean, there is easy access to the Arctic Ocean. But from the Pacific Ocean, the only route to the Arctic Ocean is the narrow Bering Strait, between Siberia (Russia) and Alaska (USA).

ARCTIC FACTS

Fourth largest **ocean** – 14,090,000 sq km;
World record for least sunshine;
Surrounded by cold **land**;
North Pole **first reached** in 1909;
At the North Pole all lines of longitude meet and every direction is **SOUTH**.

▲ *Inuit homes in Godhavn, on the west coast of Greenland. This village is called Qeqertarsuaq by the Inuit. In midsummer, most of the snow and ice has melted in this part of Greenland – but there is a big iceberg floating in the sea. These huge blocks of ice break off the ice-sheet that covers Greenland's mountains.*

▲ *Inuit (Eskimo) fishing for cod through a crack in the spring ice. He has travelled over the sea from his village by sledge. Fish are a good source of protein for families in the far north.*

WILDLIFE IN GREENLAND

Land animals have to cope with very long winters. The Arctic fox turns white for camouflage.

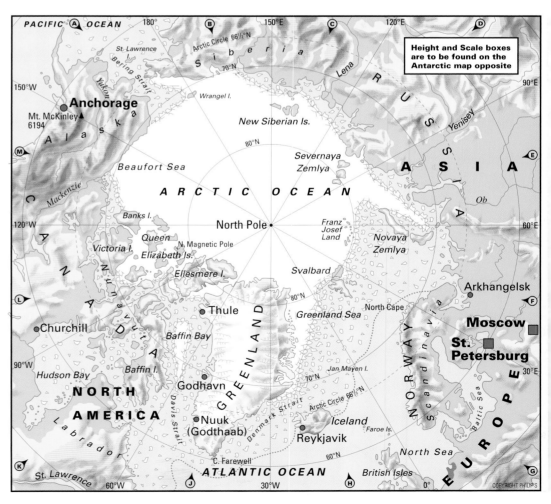

ANTARCTICA

ANTARCTICA is the continent surrounding the South Pole. It is the coldest, windiest and iciest place in the world! It is also very isolated, as the map shows.

No people live in Antarctica permanently. Scientists work in the research stations. Some are studying the effects of our climate warming up. Everything that is needed has to be brought in during the short summer. From November to January, icebreakers can reach the land, but huge icebergs are always a danger. In winter (May to July) it is always dark, the sea is frozen, and people have to face extreme cold and dangerous blizzards.

No-one 'owns' Antarctica. The Antarctic Treaty ensures that the continent should only be used for scientific research. This means it should remain peaceful for ever. The flags of the 32 nations that have signed the treaty stand in a ring round the South Pole, near the USA's Amundsen-Scott base. Even Antarctica has more and more tourists visiting the area every year.

ANTARCTICA FACTS

Fifth largest **continent** – 14,100,000 sq km;
World record for coldest temperature;
Surrounded by cold **seas**;
South Pole **first reached** in 1911;
At the South Pole all lines of longitude meet and every direction is **NORTH**.

▲ **Rookery of Gentoo Penguins in Antarctica.** *Penguins cannot fly, but they can swim very well. The parents use their feet to protect the eggs and chicks from the cold ice! No land animals live in Antarctica, but the ocean is full of fish, which provide food for penguins, seals and whales.*

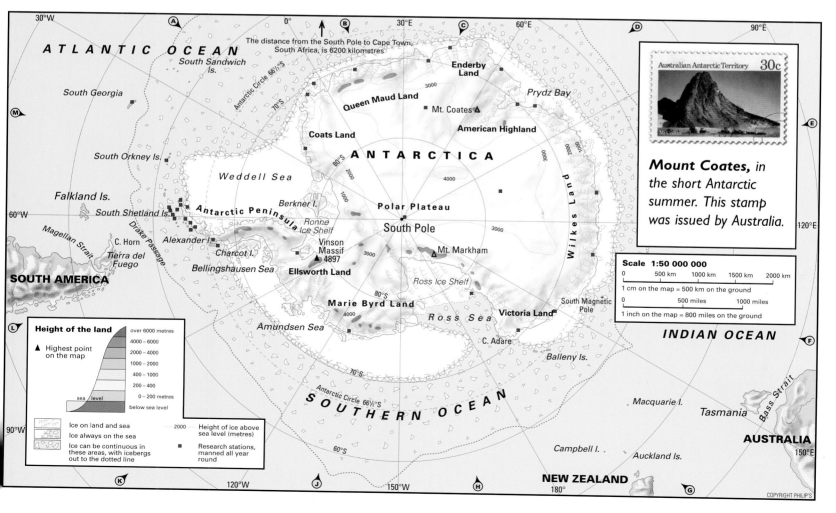

Mount Coates, in the short Antarctic summer. This stamp was issued by Australia.

The distance from the South Pole to Cape Town, South Africa, is 6200 kilometres

Scale 1:50 000 000

1 cm on the map = 500 km on the ground

1 inch on the map = 800 miles on the ground

Height of the land
▲ Highest point on the map
- over 6000 metres
- 4000 – 6000
- 2000 – 4000
- 1000 – 2000
- 400 – 1000
- 200 – 400
- 0 – 200 metres
- below sea level

Ice on land and sea
Ice always on the sea
Ice can be continuous in these areas, with icebergs out to the dotted line

2000 Height of ice above sea level (metres)
■ Research stations, manned all year round

QUIZ QUESTIONS

NAME THE COUNTRY

There is a long, thin country in almost every continent. Can you name the countries shown here – and name the continent in which they are found? (If you need help, look at pages 8–9 for a map of the countries of the world.)

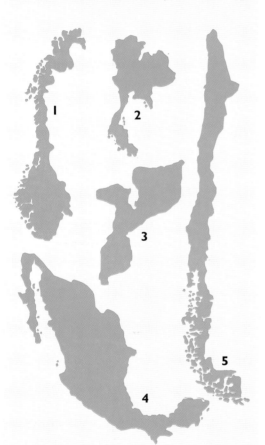

1

2

3

5

4

NAME THE ISLAND

The name of the continent where each island is found is marked on each outline. Do you know (a) the name of each island, and (b) to which country each island belongs (or are they island countries)?

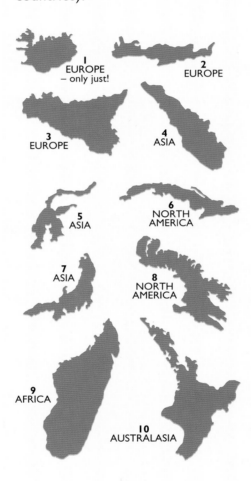

1
EUROPE
– only just!

2
EUROPE

3
EUROPE

4
ASIA

5
ASIA

6
NORTH
AMERICA

7
ASIA

8
NORTH
AMERICA

9
AFRICA

10
AUSTRALASIA

A MYSTERY MESSAGE

Use the map of the countries of the world on pages 8–9 to decode this message. Each missing word is all or part of the name of a country. (For some answers, letters have to be taken out of or added to the name of the country.)

I was _ _ _ _ a _ _ (east of Austria), so I bought a large _ _ _ _ _ _ (east of Greece), some _ _ _ _ _ ns (east of Norway) and a bottle of _ _ _ _ ugal (west of Spain). Finally, I ate an _ _ _ land (west of Norway) -cream. I enjoyed my _ e _ _ i (east of Mauritania), but afterwards I began to _ _ _ _ earia (south of Romania) and I got a bad S _ _ _ _ (south of France). A O _ _ _ (east of Saudi Arabia) told me: 'Just eat Philip _ _ _ _ sapples (south of Taiwan) and _ _ gypt (east of Libya), cooked in a Ja _ _ _ (east of Korea). Tomorrow you can eat a Ghban _ _ _ (east of Ivory Coast) and some _ _ _ _ _ _ (east of Peru) nuts. It shouldn't _ _ _ _ a Rica (west of Panama) you too much.' I said: 'You must be _ _ _ agascar (east of Mozambique)! I think I've got _ _ _ _ ysr _ _ (north of Indonesia). I'll have _ _ / _ _ (west of Benin) to a doctor quickly, otherwise I'll soon be _ _ _ _ Sea (lake between Israel and Jordan).'

Happily, the doctor _ _ bared (island country south of USA) me, so I am still M _ _ d _ _ _ s (islands west of Sri Lanka) today!

GREAT RIVERS OF EUROPE

Use pages 18–37 to discover which great river flows through or near each pair of cities.
1 Vienna (Austria) and Budapest (Hungary)
2 Rotterdam (Netherlands) and Bonn (Germany)
3 Avignon (France) and Lyons (France)
4 Worcester (England) and Gloucester (England)
5 Toledo (Spain) and Lisbon (Portugal)

PLACES IN ASIA

Move the letters to find:
Countries RAIN; CHAIN; MOAN; AWAIT N; PLANE
Capital cities ANIMAL; DIARY H; THE TANKS; A BULK; COOL MOB

FIND THE COLOUR

Each answer is a colour. Use the atlas index and the maps to help you. Cover the right-hand column with a piece of paper and try to answer the left-hand column only. Award yourself 2 points for each correct answer to the left-hand column only, or 1 point if you used the clues in both columns.

1 A sea between Egypt and Saudi Arabia . . .
2 **A big island east of Canada . . .**
3 The sea between Turkey and Ukraine . . .
4 **The sea between Korea and China . . .**
5 The sea on which Arkhangelsk lies, in Russia . . .
6 **A town in southern France which is also a fruit . . .**
7 The tributary of the River Nile that flows from Ethiopia to Khartoum (Sudan) . . .

. . . and the river on the border of Oklahoma and Texas, USA.
. . . and a bay on the west side of Lake Michigan, USA.

. . . and a forest in Germany.
. . . and a (stony) river in Wyoming, USA.
. . . and the river flowing north from Lake Victoria to Khartoum (Sudan).
. . . and the river which makes the border between South Africa and Namibia.

. . . and a mountain ridge in eastern USA.

OCEANS AND SEAS

What ocean would you cross on an aeroplane journey . . .

1 From Australia to the USA?
2 From Brazil to South Africa?
3 From Canada to Russia?
4 From Madagascar to Indonesia?
5 From Mexico to Portugal?

What sea would you cross on an aeroplane journey . . .

6 From Saudi Arabia to Egypt?
7 From Korea to Japan
8 From Denmark to the UK?
9 From Vietnam to the Philippines?
10 From Cuba to Colombia?

THINGS TO DO

COLLECT STAMPS WITH A THEME
A stamp collection soon grows. Try a thematic collection: choose a theme (topic) and collect stamps on that theme. For example, you could collect:
Holidays on stamps – such as the stamps on page 80.
Map stamps – small islands often issue map stamps to show everyone where they are!
Traditional crafts on stamps.

COLLECT YOUR OWN COINS
Ask people who have been abroad for any foreign coins they do not want – you will have an instant collection! If you cannot have the coins to keep, you could make pencil or crayon rubbings on thin paper. The coin box on page 16 is a good starting-point for making sense of the coins in your collection: each coin has a date, a value, a picture – and a country!

USA STATES QUIZ

All the answers can be found on the maps on pages 68–9 and 72–7.
* *Do NOT include Alaska and Hawaii.*

1 Which is the *biggest* state?*
2 Which is the *smallest* state?
3 Which state reaches furthest *north*? (Careful!)*
4 Which state reaches furthest *south*?*
5 Which state reaches furthest *west*?*
6 Which state reaches furthest *east*?
7 Which state is split into two by a lake?
8 Which state is split into two by an inlet of the sea?
9 Which two states are perfect rectangles in shape?
10 Which state is shaped like a saucepan?
11 In which state will you be if you visit Lake Huron?
12 In which state will you be if you visit Lake Ontario?
13 In which state will you be if you visit the Great Salt Lake?
14 In which state will you be if you visit the Mississippi delta?
15 Which state in *northern* USA is called South . . . . . ?
16 Which state in *southern* USA is called North . . . . . ?
17 There is only one place in the USA where four states meet: which states?
18 How many states have a border with Mexico?
19 How many states have a coastline on the Pacific?*
20 How many states have a coastline on the Gulf of Mexico?

ANSWERS TO ALL QUIZ QUESTIONS ARE ON PAGE 96

INDEX

HOW TO USE THIS INDEX

The first number given after each name or topic is the page number; then a letter and another number tell you which square of the map you should look at.

For example, Abidjan is in square B2 on page 57. Find B at the top or the bottom of the map on page 57 and put a finger on it. Put another finger on the number 2 at the side of the map. Move your fingers in from the edge of the map and they will meet in square B2. Abidjan will now be easy to find. It is the capital city of the Ivory Coast, a country in West Africa.

Town names are indexed to the square in which the town symbol falls. However, if the name of a physical feature goes through more than one square, the square given in the index is the one in which the biggest part of the name falls.

Names like Gulf of Mexico and Cape Horn are in the Index as 'Mexico, Gulf of' and 'Horn, Cape'.

ANSWERS TO QUESTIONS

Page 4 Atlantic Ocean; Indian Ocean; South America; Brazil.

Page 6 Vicuña in the Andes of Argentina, South America.

Page 8 Stamp from France. 'RF' stands for *République Française*.

Page 8 UN flag: olive branches for peace; map of the world with North Pole at centre.

Page 18 Brussels, Belgium: it was the headquarters of the European Union.

Page 18 Island = Iceland; Helvetia = Switzerland; Romana = Romania; España = Spain.

Page 19 Norge = Norway; Slovensko = Slovak Republic; Magyar = Hungary; Slovenija = Slovenia; Hellas = Greece.

Page 22 The London landmarks featured on the stamp are (*from left to right*): Westminster Abbey; Nelson's Column (in Trafalgar Square); statue of Eros (in Piccadilly Circus); Telecom Tower; clock tower of the Houses of Parliament (containing the bell Big Ben); St Paul's Cathedral; Tower Bridge; White Tower of the Tower of London.

Page 24 Left coin: Belgium (King). Centre: Luxembourg (Grand Duke). Right: Netherlands (Queen Beatrix).

Page 24 The yellow objects are CLOGS. They are shoes made out of wood. Very few Dutch people still wear clogs, but tourists like to buy them.

Page 26 The photograph of the fruit stall shows: a watermelon, strawberries, blackberries, mangoes, pineapples, melons, cherries, avocados, tomatoes, apricots, peaches and nectarines.

Pages 38–39 The script reads *across* the two pages: **1** Australia; **2** Egypt; **3** Hong Kong; **4** United States; **5** Taiwan.

Page 39 The five countries which share the shoreline of the Caspian Sea are Russia, Kazakhstan, Turkmenistan, Iran and Azerbaijan.

Page 40 The 15 'new' countries formed at the break-up of the USSR are (*from largest to smallest*): Russia, Kazakhstan, Ukraine, Turkmenistan, Uzbekistan, Belarus, Kyrgyzstan, Tajikistan, Azerbaijan, Georgia, Lithuania, Latvia, Estonia, Moldova and Armenia.

Page 41 Khabarovsk is on the River Amur. Moskva (= Moscow) to Vladivostok.

Page 44 Clockwise (*from the top right-hand corner*): samosas, ground coriander, coriander leaves, cumin, pakoras, rice, poppadums, red chilli powder next to yellow turmeric powder, green okra (also called 'ladies fingers'), garlic and bay leaves.

Page 50 These decorations are lanterns, made out of paper.

Page 65 Australia, of course!

Page 68 The north shores of Lakes Superior, Huron, Erie and Ontario are in Canada, and the south shores are in the USA. Lake Michigan is entirely in the USA.

Page 69 El Salvador only has a coastline on the Pacific Ocean. Belize only has a coastline on the Caribbean Sea. (Honduras has a tiny coastline on the Pacific – look closely at the map!) One island has two countries on it: Haiti and Dominican Republic.

Page 73 Seattle to Miami is 5445 kilometres; New Orleans to Chicago is 1488 kilometres.

Page 76 The Spanish words mean: Amarillo = Yellow; Colorado = Coloured; El Paso = The pass; Los Angeles = The angels; San José = St Joseph; San Francisco = St Francis.

Page 81 Aruba and Curaçao are owned by the Netherlands; Turks Is, Caicos I., Grand Cayman, Anguilla and Montserrat are owned by the UK. The islands of Guadeloupe and Martinique are both part of France. Some of the Virgin Islands belong to the UK, and some belong to the USA. The island of Hispaniola is shared by Haiti and the Dominican Republic.

QUIZ ANSWERS
(on pages 90–91)

NAME THE COUNTRY
1 Norway (Europe)
2 Thailand (Asia)
3 Mozambique (Africa)
4 Mexico (Central America)
5 Chile (South America)

NAME THE ISLAND
1 Iceland
2 Crete (Greece)
3 Sicily (Italy)
4 Sumatra (Indonesia)
5 Sulawesi (Indonesia)
6 Cuba
7 Honshu (Japan)
8 Baffin Island (Canada)
9 Madagascar
10 North Island (New Zealand)

A MYSTERY MESSAGE
I was *hungry*, so I bought a large *turkey*, some *swedes* and a bottle of *port*. Finally, I ate an *ice*-cream. I enjoyed my *meal*, but afterwards I began to *bulge* and I got a bad *pain*. A man told me: 'Just eat *pine*apples and *egg* cooked in a *pan*. Tomorrow you can eat a *banana* and some *Brazil* nuts. It shouldn't *cost* you too much.' I said: 'You must be *mad*! I think I've got *malaria*. I'll have *to go* to a doctor quickly, otherwise I'll soon be *dead*.'

Happily, the doctor *cured* me, so I am still *alive* today!

GREAT RIVERS OF EUROPE
1 Danube; 2 Rhine; 3 Rhône; 4 Severn; 5 Tagus.

PLACES IN ASIA
Countries
Iran; China; Oman; Taiwan; Nepal.
Capital cities
Manila; Riyadh; Tashkent; Kabul; Colombo.

COLOUR QUIZ
1 Red (Red Sea/Red River)
2 Green (Greenland/Green Bay)
3 Black (Black Sea/Black Forest)
4 Yellow (Yellow Sea/Yellowstone River)
5 White (White Sea/White Nile)
6 Orange (Orange/Orange River)
7 Blue (Blue Nile/Blue Ridge)

STATES OF THE USA
1 Texas
2 Rhode Island
3 Minnesota
4 Florida
5 Washington
6 Maine
7 Michigan
8 Maryland
9 Wyoming and Colorado
10 Oklahoma
11 Michigan
12 New York
13 Utah
14 Louisiana
15 South Dakota
16 North Carolina
17 Utah, Colorado, Arizona and New Mexico
18 Four (California, Arizona, New Mexico and Texas)
19 Three (Washington, Oregon and California)
20 Five (Texas, Louisiana, Mississippi, Alabama and Florida)

OCEANS AND SEAS
1 Pacific; 2 Atlantic; 3 Arctic; 4 Indian; 5 Atlantic; 6 Red Sea; 7 Sea of Japan; 8 North Sea; 9 South China Sea; 10 Caribbean Sea.

PICTURE ACKNOWLEDGEMENTS

Sue Atkinson 66 bottom centre; **BBC Natural History Unit** /Keith Scholey 58 bottom left; **Colorsport** 22 centre right; **Corbis** /Tiziana & Gianni Baldizzone 20 centre, /Philip James Corwin 11 right, /Richard Cummins 74 bottom, /Duomo 72 top, /Kevin Fleming 49 left, /Free Agents Limited 20 top, /Jason Hawkes 22 bottom left, /Jason Hosking/zefa 50 bottom right, /David Katzenstein 85, /Charles & Josette Lenars 11 left, /Yang Liu 49 right, /Stephanie Maze 83, /Bruno Morandi/ Robert Harding World Imagery 48 centre right, /Carl & Ann Purcell 75 bottom, /Patrick Robert/Sygma 51, /Dietrich Rose/zefa 19 centre, /Bill Ross 74 centre, /Royalty-Free 13, 19 right, 48 left /Tony Waltham/Robert Harding World Imagery 88 top, /Nik Wheeler 54 bottom right, 68, /Michael S. Yamashita 50 centre; **Finnish Tourist Board** 20 bottom right; **Robert Harding Picture Library** 14, 22 centre left, 28 centre right, 30 centre right, 30 bottom, 41 middle centre, 43 left, 44 top, 46 top, 64 centre left, 64 centre right, 70 top, 70 bottom left, 70 bottom right, 79, 80 top, 80 bottom left, 81 left, 82, 86 top, 24 bottom centre, 34 bottom left, 36 centre right, 48 top, 66 top left, 22 top, /David Beatty 40 bottom left, /P. Bordes 56 top, /C. Bowman 32 centre, 78 top, /Rob Cousins 26 right, 46 bottom right, /Nigel Francis 26 centre left, /Simon Harris 77 top, /Kim Hart 19 left, /Gavin Hellier 77 bottom, /F. Jackson 12 top, /Carol Jopp 15 right, /Thomas Laird 45 bottom, /Louise Murray 25, /Roy Rainford 23, 33, 74 top, /Geoff Renner 55, 87 top, 89, /Christopher Rennie 84 bottom right, /Michael Short 34 top right, /J. H. C. Wilson 45 top, /Nick Wood 66 bottom left; **James Hughes** 22 bottom right; **Hulton Deutsch Collection** 54 bottom left; **Hutchison Library** 24 centre, 40 centre bottom, /Sarah Errington 58 top, /Tony Souter 30 centre left, 32; **Image Bank** 24 top, /Gallant 42 top, /L. D. Gordon 87 bottom, /Bullaty Lomeo 36 top right, /Michael Melford 32 top, /Kaz Mori 75 top, /Jeffrey M. Spielman 8, /Harald Sund 40 top right, /Hans Wolf 28 top right, 28 bottom left; **Nina Jenkins** 54 centre, 56 centre right; **Steve Nevill** 76 bottom; **NPA Group** /5 top left, 5 top right, 5 bottom left, 5 bottom right; **Panos Pictures** /Gary John Norman 57 left; **Planet Earth Pictures** 60 top, /G. Cafiero 43 right, /John Eastcott 76 centre, 6, 88 below, /John Lythgoe 78 centre right, /John Waters/Bernadette Spiegel 39 top; **Octopus Publishing Group Ltd** /Graham Kirk 78 bottom left, /Paul Williams 46 bottom centre; **Russia & Republics Photolibrary** /Mark Wadlow 40 bottom right, 41 top; **Science Photo Library** /European Space Agency 4, /John Mead 63; **Still Pictures** /Chris Caldicott 53, 54 top, /Mark Edwards 56 bottom left, 84 bottom, /Michel Gunther 58 bottom centre, /John Maier 10 top, 61, /Roland Seitre 62; **Tony Stone Images** 28 bottom centre, 50 top, 66 bottom right, /Doug Armand 67 top, /John Beatty 86 bottom, /Stephen Beer 60 bottom left, /Richard Bradbury 69, /Suzanne & Nick Geary 64 centre, 76 top, /Walter Geierserger 29, /George Grigoriou 34 bottom right, 35 top, /Gavin Hellier 36 bottom left, /Dave Jacobs 72 bottom, /H. Richard Johnston 71, /Hideo Kurihara 64 top, /Alain le Garsmeur 48 bottom, 60 bottom right, /John Noble 84 bottom centre, /Nicholas Parfitt 59, /Pete Seaward 30 top, /Ed Simpson 84 top, /Nabeel Turner 42 bottom right, 50 bottom left, /Trevor Wood 44 left; **Judy Todd** 38 top right; **David & Jill Wright** 10 bottom, 15 left, 16, 18, 20 bottom left, 21, 24 bottom right, 26 top left, 26 top right, 37, 42 bottom left, 44 centre, 46 bottom left, 52 bottom, 57 right, 58 bottom right, 60 bottom centre, 67 bottom, 81 right.